Dynamic Devotions for Teens

by Marvin Osborn

Ephesians Four Ministries
CHURCH GROWTH INSTITUTE
P.O. Box 7, Elkton, MD 21922-0007

Editor: Cindy G. Spear
Editorial & Design Assistant: Tamara Johnson

ISBN 0-941005-90-9

Printed in the United States by
Morris Publishing
3212 East Highway 30
Kearney, NE 68847
1-800-650-7888

Contents

How to Have Dynamic Devotions..5

Why Daily Devotions?..6

Taking a Stand..8

Let's Talk about Sex 10

Commitment..12

What Does Stewardship Really Mean?..14

The Will of God..16

Why Do Bad Things Happen to Good People?..18

Your Thought Life..20

Salvation..22

Friends..24

Love..26

Thou Shalt Not Covet 28

Thou Shalt Not Steal 30

Thou Shalt Have No Other Gods 32

Thou Shalt Not Take the Name of the Lord Thy God in Vain 34

Does Lying REALLY Hurt?..36

Hatred = Murder..38

"Missionary" Dating..40

Life and Death..42

Independent but under Authority..44

Abortion 46

Reach Out and Invite Someone..48

Just Give Me Some Rock and Roll Music 50

Thou Shalt Not Commit Adultery..52

Suicide 54

Honor Thy Father and Mother..56

Temptation 58

Guys: What to Look for in a Christian Girl..60

Girls: What to Look for in a Christian Guy..62

The Do's and Don'ts of Dating..64

More Do's and Don'ts of Dating.. 66

Dress for Success.. 68

Money: How Do You Manage It?.. 70

Building a Barrier against Sin... 72

Forgiveness... 74

Sons and Daughters of God 76

Drugs and Alcohol... 78

Are We Living in the Last Days? 80

Self-Esteem 82

A Father to the Fatherless 84

Mistakes – Starting Over 86

How Do We Love God?.. 88

Love Your Neighbor As Yourself... 90

How to Lead Others to Christ 92

How to Lead Others to Christ, Part 2....................................... 94

Why Do the Wicked Prosper? 96

Situation Ethics: What's Right and What's Wrong? 98

Formula for Christian Success 100

Prayer 102

Balancing Your Life.. 104

Balancing Your Life, Part 2... 106

Don't Give Up 108

Prayer Guide 111

Sunday.. 112

Monday 113

Tuesday 114

Wednesday 115

Thursday 116

Friday 117

Saturday... 118

How to Have Dynamic Devotions

God knew thousands of years ago what areas in your life you would struggle with, and He provided guidance in the Bible to help you through those trials. The Bible is also a blueprint for our lives, teaching us through example and giving us principles to live by, while showing us who Christ is and what Christianity is. We are privileged to spend time in God's Word each day.

I remember the first time I had devotions back in 1978. I attended a fall retreat at a camp and noticed that everyone took time each morning to read the Bible and pray. I did not know what to do, so I simply turned to Proverbs 22:1-2. I read the verses, thought about them, and prayed that God would always purpose in my heart to seek a good reputation instead of wealth. That was it – my first devotion.

Since that time, I have determined to spend time in God's Word each day. I am a morning person, so it is easier for me to get up early and have my devotions. Several years ago while reading Joshua 1:8 about meditating on God's Word day and night, I started spending time in God's Word in the morning *and* at night. Daily devotions are a godly habit I started as a teen and a habit I want to pass on to you.

How to Have Dynamic Devotions

1. Find a book like *Dynamic Devotions for Teens* to use as a guide for your devotions.
2. Read the week's illustration each day and the verses provided.
3. Ask yourself:
   - Does the passage make any promises to me?
   - Does the passage tell of sin I should avoid?
   - Do I have areas in my life that I should give over to God to obtain those promises and/or have victory over sin?
4. Summarize the passage in the space provided.
5. Write down how you are going to apply these verses to your life.
6. Confess any sin and pray that God will give you victory over these sins and/or help you obtain the promises contained in the passage.
7. Turn to the prayer section of the devotional and pray for the requests for that day.

That is all you have to do to have a dynamic devotional life. I pray that this year you will purpose in your heart to spend time with God in the Bible and in prayer at least one time a day. It is a godly habit that will guide you all the days of your life and as Joshua 1:8 says, "This book of the law shall not depart out of thy mouth; but thou shalt meditate therein day and night, that thou mayest observe to do according to all that is written therein: for then thou shalt make thy way prosperous, and thou shalt have good success."

Why Daily Devotions?

How refreshing and encouraging it is to wake up every morning and read God's precious Word. Imagine when you read the Old Testament that our heros in the New Testament also read it over 2,000 years ago. Can you imagine the apostle Paul, Peter or Timothy rising up early and reading the same Scripture that you are reading?! What an awesome thought!

Think about all the great Christians in history, Martin Luther, Hudson Taylor, Charles Finney, Charles Spurgeon, Billy Graham ... the list goes on of great people who spent time every day in God's Word.

These people learned a very important principle of the Christian life found in Joshua 1:8, "This book of the law shall not depart out of my mouth; but thou shalt meditate therein day and night, that thou mayest observe to do according to all that is written therein: for then thou shalt make thy way prosperous, and then thou shalt have good success." Do you want to know why the people listed above were successful in their Christian walk, in their family lives, and in their ministry to others? They spent time in God's Word every day.

I started having daily devotions about 15 years ago. It has been one of the main guides for keeping me from sin, directing my life, helping me find a wonderful wife, and raising precious children.

Why is reading the Bible so important? Because God knows the needs of mankind. He knows the temptations we go through. He knows that we need godly examples of those who have succeeded in their walk and examples of those who failed in their walk. The Bible is God's Word to guide you in all areas of life.

Do you want to be successful? Do you want to be the next Billy Graham or Charles Finney? You may not grow up to be a "super" evangelist, "super" preacher or a "super" teacher, but if you spend time in God's Word daily, and follow and apply all of the principles taught in His Word, you will reach your full life's potential. Determine in your heart this week to begin the godly habit of having daily devotions.

Sunday _____ Read _Psalm 1_____
　　　　　　　(Date)

Summarize the Passage_____

_____

How does it apply to my life? _____

Monday _____ Read _Josh. 1:8-9_____
　　　　　　　(Date)

Summarize the Passage_____

_____

How does it apply to my life? _____

Tuesday _____ Read _Ps. 119:97-104_____
　　　　　　　(Date)

Summarize the Passage_____

_____

How does it apply to my life? _____

Wednesday_____ Read _Ps. 119:105-112____
　　　　　　　(Date)

Summarize the Passage_____

_____

How does it apply to my life? _____

Thursday _____ Read _2 Tim. 3:12-17_____
　　　　　　　(Date)

Summarize the Passage_____

_____

How does it apply to my life? _____

Friday_____ Read _Heb. 4:12_____
　　　　　　　(Date)

Summarize the Passage_____

_____

How does it apply to my life? _____

Saturday_____ Read _Ps. 119:9-16_____
　　　　　　　(Date)

Summarize the Passage_____

_____

How does it apply to my life? _____

Taking a Stand

"Stand Up, Stand Up for Jesus ye soldiers of the cross..." Those words from the great hymn have brought strength to Christians who are weathering the storm of persecution or temptation, and conviction to those who failed that same test.

A good friend of mind was returning home to Maryland from Bible college out west when he stopped in a diner for supper. He was sitting there alone when he heard a loud-mouthed man behind him blaspheming God. He turned and saw that the man had not only a big mouth but also a big body to go with it. The man continued to curse God and finally said he would beat up any Christians in the place. He yelled, "Are there any *&^%$@! Christians in this diner?" Instead of confronting the man, my friend paid his bill and walked out of the diner.

That event happened over 20 years ago but my friend has never forgiven himself for not saying, "Yes, I'm a Christian, how may I help you?" to the loud-mouthed man.

Many of us face similar situations each day. Sure we are not usually threatened with violence if we let people know about Christ, but we face humility and even the loss of friends.

Someone once said, "If you don't stand for something, you'll fall for anything." For the Christian we should say, "If you don't stand for Christ, you'll fail at everything." Jesus said in Matthew 10:32, "Whosoever therefore shall confess me before men, him will I confess also before my Father which is in heaven." Have you taken a stand for Christ?

This week as you do your devotions, think about the people you read about in the Bible. How could they have done things differently? Also, think about my friend. If you were put into that situation, how would you react? Finally, think about your life – are there situations in your life where you need to take a stand for Jesus?

Sunday _March 26_ Read _Matt. 10:32-33_
(Date)

Summarize the Passage _whoever accepts Jesus as his savior_
will be let into heaven but whoever doesn't accept Him won't

How does it apply to my life? _I need to spread the word out_
about my savior

Monday _March 27_ Read _Rom. 10:9-13_
(Date)

Summarize the Passage _you need to confess to the Lord that_
He is the One and you will be saved everyone can do it

How does it apply to my life? _I need to do a good job_
telling everyone God doesn't single anyone out

Tuesday _March 28_ Read _Rom. 10:14-18_
(Date)

Summarize the Passage _We need to bring the_
gospel to others, they won't wa. it unless we tell them

How does it apply to my life? _school_

Wednesday _____ Read _Luke 22:54-62_
(Date)

Summarize the Passage _____

How does it apply to my life? _____

Thursday _____ Read _Daniel 3_
(Date)

Summarize the Passage _____

How does it apply to my life? _____

Friday _____ Read _2 Tim. 2:11-13_
(Date)

Summarize the Passage _____

How does it apply to my life? _____

Saturday _____ Read _Acts 2:14-21_
(Date)

Summarize the Passage _____

How does it apply to my life? _____

Let's Talk about Sex

Everyone is talking about sex! Have you ever heard the phrase "sex sells"? Sex is used to sell music, cars, beer, computers, jeans, and everything in between. You cannot turn on a radio or television without seeing or hearing sex used to sell products in commercials, sex being the central focus on a sitcom or sex being the central theme of a song. Sex sells!

Unfortunately, what sex is selling is sin. The Centers for Disease Control estimate that there are a million cases of HIV infection nationwide, sexually transmitted diseases infect three million teenagers annually, unwed pregnancies have increased 87 percent among 15- to 19-year-olds, and abortions among teens have risen 67 percent since 1970.

I graduated from a Christian high school with a boy named James. For years he heard the Bible messages, memorized verses, and sang in the school choir, yet because of his home life and the friends he associated with he soon shunned his Christian beliefs seeking what the world had to offer. Just six years after graduation James died of AIDS. Today, James is buried near the Christian high school from which he graduated. What James failed to realize was that just because this world is selling you sex, you don't have to buy into it. Unfortunately, James bought into it and died.

The fact is that many Christian teenagers, just like James, buy into this lifestyle philosophy and end up experiencing the product of that sin which the Bible says eventually ends in death.

This week as you read the Bible passages provided, think about James and the people you know who have sought this world's pleasures and ended up pregnant, in jail or even dead in their pursuit of those pleasures. Are you buying into the sex lies this world is selling? What things are you doing that violate God's Word? What things are you going to do to change these activities?

Sunday _____ Read _Gal. 5:19-23_____
               (Date)

Summarize the Passage_____

_____

How does it apply to my life? _____

Monday _____ Read _2 Tim. 2:22-26_____
               (Date)

Summarize the Passage_____

_____

How does it apply to my life? _____

Tuesday _____ Read _1 Cor. 5:9-13_____
               (Date)

Summarize the Passage_____

_____

How does it apply to my life? _____

Wednesday _____ Read _1 Cor. 6:9-12_____
               (Date)

Summarize the Passage_____

_____

How does it apply to my life? _____

Thursday _____ Read _1 Cor. 6:13-18_____
               (Date)

Summarize the Passage_____

_____

How does it apply to my life? _____

Friday _____ Read _Eph. 5:1-8_____
               (Date)

Summarize the Passage_____

_____

How does it apply to my life? _____

Saturday _____ Read _1 Thess. 4:3-4_____
               (Date)

Summarize the Passage_____

_____

How does it apply to my life? _____

Commitment

Technology is unbelievable. Most people don't realize that when our ancestors set out to go to California from Boston by covered wagon the trip took *six months*. Today that same trip takes only a few days by car and just a few hours by plane.

When our ancestors decided to relocate to California it took REAL commitment. They realized that if the trip was going to take six months, and that because of the hazards faced on such a trip, that they may never see their family or Boston again. Yet, they took that challenge and ventured into the unknown.

We live in a world of transcontinental travel, microwave ovens, around the clock news, and television. Dinner which used to take hours to make can be delivered to your door in 30 minutes. Everything we could have ever imagined 30 years ago can just about be instantaneously obtained by picking the phone.

As fabulous as this sounds, the problem is that we have no commitment anymore. In today's society anything that takes more than a couple of hours to do is a major commitment. Thus we see society as a whole in trouble because husbands and wives are no longer committed to each other, teenagers are no longer committed to their families, families are no longer committed to church, and Christians are no longer committed to God.

Commitment is a part of life, and especially a part of our Christian walk. This week as you read your Bible passages, meditate on the commitment each individual had and the price they paid for that commitment. Do you have that kind of commitment? What areas of your life do you need help with in building up your commitment?

Sunday _____ Read Dan. 6:4-10 _____
(Date)

Summarize the Passage_____

_____

How does it apply to my life? _____

Monday _____ Read Dan. 6:11-17 _____
(Date)

Summarize the Passage_____

_____

How does it apply to my life? _____

Tuesday _____ Read Dan. 6:18-24 _____
(Date)

Summarize the Passage_____

_____

How does it apply to my life? _____

Wednesday _____ Read Heb. 11:32-40 _____
(Date)

Summarize the Passage_____

_____

How does it apply to my life? _____

Thursday _____ Read Dan. 3:8-18 _____
(Date)

Summarize the Passage_____

_____

How does it apply to my life? _____

Friday _____ Read Dan. 3:19-25 _____
(Date)

Summarize the Passage_____

_____

How does it apply to my life? _____

Saturday _____ Read Dan. 3:26-30 _____
(Date)

Summarize the Passage_____

_____

How does it apply to my life? _____

Commitment

What Does Stewardship Really Mean?

As a teen I thought the word stewardship was just a fancy word for giving. After all, most churches have stewardship drives that center around giving above and beyond your tithes.

In the Scriptures stewardship is not just giving but pertains to how we live our entire life. God cares that you attend church and give your tithes faithfully, but He also cares how you spend the rest of your time, talent, and money. The term *stewardship* relates to every part of your life.

Consider this, God owns everything and as owner He commands us to give the first 10 percent (the tithe) of our earnings to Him and expects us to manage the other 90 percent. We can spend the money as we like as long as it doesn't violate Scripture. We will have to one day answer to how we spend that money. Does that mean we can't spend money on arcade games — no. It does mean that if the money you spent on arcade games was supposed to be spent on your brother's birthday present or given as an offering in church, you were wrong.

In the same way that God commanded the tithe, He commands us to attend church. He does not tell us how to spend the rest of the week. If that week is spent on self-indulgent behavior with no time for your devotions, prayer and concern for others — you are wrong. God has also blessed each of us with special talents and spiritual gifts. Some Christians only use their talents and gifts in the workplace to make money instead of also allowing God to use those talents and gifts to minister to others.

What most people don't realize is that God doesn't need our money or our time or our talents to do the work of the church. He chooses to use these things to build the church. When we don't utilize our time, talent, and money the way God intends us to use them, we display a selfish attitude, an attitude that calls for repentence.

Is it wrong to spend a restful Sunday afternoon watching television, or buying a new pair of shoes for ourselves, or using my Spiritual gift in the church and at school to help others? Of course not! God wants each of us to live a full, balanced life. As we go about our daily lives, we need to be sensitive to the needs of others and the Holy Spirit's leading in our lives. If we are fulfilling God's known will in our lives (church attendance, tithing, using our talents and gifts in the church) and are sensitive to and seek to meet the physical and mental needs of others, then we are good stewards. This week, examine your life in light of what God says about stewardship. How does your life compare? What areas need improvement? What are you going to do about it?

Sunday _____ Read _Matt. 19:16-26_____
(Date)

Summarize the Passage_____

_____

How does it apply to my life? _____

Monday _____ Read _Luke 16:10-13_____
(Date)

Summarize the Passage_____

_____

How does it apply to my life? _____

Tuesday _____ Read _Matt. 3:10-12_____
(Date)

Summarize the Passage_____

_____

How does it apply to my life? _____

Wednesday _____ Read _Prov. 24:29-34_____
(Date)

Summarize the Passage_____

_____

How does it apply to my life? _____

Thursday _____ Read _Luke 16:1-2_____
(Date)

Summarize the Passage_____

_____

How does it apply to my life? _____

Friday_____ Read _Prov. 30:24-28_____
(Date)

Summarize the Passage_____

_____

How does it apply to my life? _____

Saturday_____ Read _1 Cor. 12:1-11_____
(Date)

Summarize the Passage_____

_____

How does it apply to my life? _____

The Will of God

Hundreds of books and thousands of Christians have addressed the subject of how to find God's will for our life. We somehow believe that God has this mysterious plan for each of us and it is our job to find out that will. Much of my early Christian life was filled with thinking God's will was like a tightrope wire. We spend our time balancing our lives on that rope, and if we sway from the rope we sway from God's will.

Fortunately neither theory is true. What a terrible trick God would be playing if we had to desperately search out His will for our lives or if His will were so narrow for our lives that if we take a wrong turn, somehow we are never able to recover.

God has actually two plans for your life the known and the unknown. The known will of God is found in the word of God. It is the will of God for all Christians to obey the commandments and principles taught in the Bible.

The unknown will of God is somewhat more complicated. I like to picture God's unknown will as a football field. God has blessed me with certain talents and Spiritual gifts that I am supposed to use throughout my life. As long as I do not step out of bounds (sin), and I am using those talents and gifts to obey the known will of God, I'm in the will of God. Every once in a while God will send in a play (or redirect what I'm doing) to help me become a more effective player.

The question always comes up, what if I fall into sin — can I ever be in God's will again? First, you must obey God's known will and examine yourself to see if you are really saved. Then you need to ask forgiveness of God, and of the family and friends you may have hurt. God's perfect will for your life may have been hampered but is not lost. Your role on the football team may have changed from the quarterback to the offensive lineman. You may never be the one who leads millions of people to Christ, like a Billy Graham, but you might be the one inviting people to come hear Billy speak.

That's why it is so important to keep God's known will for your life. You need to keep yourself from sin so that you can be more effectively used of God throughout your life. Someone once said, "You will never know God's unknown will until you start obeying His known will." Your job is to discover and follow God's known will. He will reveal His unknown to you in due time. This week, discover God's known will for your life. Are you obeying His will? What things do you need to do to obey His will?

Sunday _____ Read <u>Rom. 12:1-2</u>
(Date)

Summarize the Passage_____

_____

How does it apply to my life? _____

Monday _____ Read <u>2 Peter 3:9; 1 Tim. 2:1-6</u>
(Date)

Summarize the Passage_____

_____

How does it apply to my life? _____

Tuesday _____ Read <u>1 Thess. 4:1-4</u>
(Date)

Summarize the Passage_____

_____

How does it apply to my life? _____

Wednesday _____ Read <u>1 Thess. 5:18</u>
(Date)

Summarize the Passage_____

_____

How does it apply to my life? _____

Thursday _____ Read <u>John 6:39-40</u>
(Date)

Summarize the Passage_____

_____

How does it apply to my life? _____

Friday _____ Read <u>Ex. 20:1-11</u>
(Date)

Summarize the Passage_____

_____

How does it apply to my life? _____

Saturday _____ Read <u>Ex. 20:12-17</u>
(Date)

Summarize the Passage_____

_____

How does it apply to my life? _____

The Will of God

Why Do Bad Things Happen to Good People?

All of us know seemingly godly people who have suffered tremendously in their lives. I know a deacon whose wife has suffered four miscarriages. Aren't Christians supposed to be immune to suffering?

Too many Christians have taken hold of that philosophy. When we hear testimonies of how people get saved 99 percent of the time we are left with a "they lived happily ever after" ending. Unfortunately that is not how life is. Christians throughout the history of time have had to suffer. Here are a few examples of those who suffered in the Bible:

1. Job suffered financial, social, and emotional loss and suffered physical health problems.

2. Abraham and Sarah suffered the humiliation of being childless (in the Old Testament days children were a sign of God's blessing) for close to 100 years before God gave them a child.

3. Christ suffered more than anyone so that you and I could receive salvation.

Suffering is as natural to the life of the Christian as the blessings we live for. You should expect to suffer in your lifetime. Basically we suffer for four reasons:

1. Suffering is used to convict of sin.

2. Suffering helps teach us humility and brings us closer to God.

3. Suffering allows God to work in our lives (Abraham and Sarah).

4. Enduring suffering brings glory to God (Christ).

Quite frankly we may never know why we go through particular periods of suffering in our lives, but we know that if we are yielded to Christ He will give us strength and guide us through it. Have you suffered before? Do you know someone who is going through a period of suffering? This week as you read the passages provided, think about how you can help that person who is suffering. What plan of action can you take to help alleviate their burden?

Sunday _____ Read <u>Heb. 11:32-40</u>
      (Date)

Summarize the Passage_____

_____

How does it apply to my life? _____

Monday _____ Read <u>2 Tim. 2:1-13</u>
      (Date)

Summarize the Passage_____

_____

How does it apply to my life? _____

Tuesday _____ Read <u>2 Tim. 2:10-14</u>
      (Date)

Summarize the Passage_____

_____

How does it apply to my life? _____

Wednesday _____ Read <u>James 1:1-5</u>
      (Date)

Summarize the Passage_____

_____

How does it apply to my life? _____

Thursday _____ Read <u>1 Peter 1:6-9</u>
      (Date)

Summarize the Passage_____

_____

How does it apply to my life? _____

Friday_____ Read <u>Ps. 66:10-12</u>
      (Date)

Summarize the Passage_____

_____

How does it apply to my life? _____

Saturday_____ Read <u>1 Peter 4:12-19</u>
      (Date)

Summarize the Passage_____

_____

How does it apply to my life? _____

Your Thought Life

A person's thought life is probably the most personal thing anyone possesses. No one really knows what you spend your time thinking about, no one *really* knows your innermost secrets – except God.

So many things affect the way we think. I heard someone say that our brains are like computers. If we put garbage in, we'll get garbage out. We think that when the Bible says "what we sow we shall also reap" that we are punished immediately for the sins we commit. Nothing could be more wrong! When we continue to put garbage in our minds we may not see that garbage come out until many years later when faced with a moment of temptation.

There's a hot new term in the counseling field called *sexual addicts*. Some of our most well-known movie and rock stars have put themselves under a rehabilitation program to help them overcome this "addiction." Do you think that these people woke up one day and suddenly became addicted to sex? No, in all probability they spent hours thinking, reading, watching, and participating in sexual perversion.

What kind of things could be classified as garbage in our lives:

1. Pornography: explicit magazines, explicit movies or television shows, explicit posters and books, romance novels, etc.

2. Music: sexually or violently suggestive music.

3. Dirty jokes or conversations: Although they may be funny, they are not pleasing to God.

4. Rumors: idle gossip and rumors cause you to think negatively about others.

You could probably name a few more things that could be classified as garbage. This week as you read the passages about our thought life, examine how you think. Are your thoughts consistently on sin? Would you be embarrassed if others could somehow read your mind? Remember God can read your mind. What are you going to do about cleaning up the way you think?

Sunday _____ Read _Prov. 23:7, 12_____
               (Date)

Summarize the Passage_____

_____

How does it apply to my life? _____

Monday _____ Read _1 Cor. 10:12-15_____
               (Date)

Summarize the Passage_____

_____

How does it apply to my life? _____

Tuesday _____ Read _Phil. 3:4-6_____
               (Date)

Summarize the Passage_____

_____

How does it apply to my life? _____

Wednesday_____ Read _Rom. 12:3-8_____
               (Date)

Summarize the Passage_____

_____

How does it apply to my life? _____

Thursday _____ Read _Phil. 4:8-9_____
               (Date)

Summarize the Passage_____

_____

How does it apply to my life? _____

Friday_____ Read _Gal. 5:22-24_____
               (Date)

Summarize the Passage_____

_____

How does it apply to my life? _____

Saturday_____ Read _2 Cor. 10:1-5_____
               (Date)

Summarize the Passage_____

_____

How does it apply to my life? _____

Your Thought Life

Salvation

In the early 1980s a plane leaving National Airport in Washington, D.C., crashed into the icy waters of the Potomac River. Many people lost their lives. One man standing on the shore jumped in to help a person who was struggling to make it to the shoreline. Once he helped that person he jumped back in to help someone else. Imagine someone risking his own life by jumping in those icy waters to save total strangers. Many people would have called this man a hero or even a savior. Unfortunately this man died trying to help others live.

This tragic story is a good illustration of what Christ did for us. Imagine Christ, the King of Kings, looking down from heaven and in pity seeing mankind struggling under the weight of sin with no possible way of saving ourselves and deciding to leave heaven to suffer and die, then rise from the dead to save us from our sins. What an awesome display of God's compassionate and merciful love for you and me.

Someone once said that the distance between heaven and hell is only 18 inches. That's the distance between your head and your heart. Too many people play a game called Christianity. They claim that they are Christians; they believe they may have walked an aisle when they were younger and said a prayer, but in their heart they are not sure if they are really saved or not.

Some people rely on attending church and good works, believing that they can find their own way to heaven. But the fact is that Jesus said, "I am the way, the truth, and the life: no man cometh to the Father, but by me" (John 14:6).

Many people know about Christ and what He did on the cross almost 2,000 years ago — but few have ever accepted Him as their Lord and Savior. Do you know Christ as your Lord and Savior? Have you ever asked Christ to forgive you of your sins and come and live inside you? If you haven't, contact your youth pastor today and ask him to show you how to accept Christ. This week as you study the passages provided for you, I want you to think about the precious gift of salvation Christ provided for you and the price He paid to give it to you. Do you have friends who don't know Christ? This week find an interesting way to share Christ with one of your lost friends.

Sunday _____ Read <u>Rom. 3:23; 6:23; Isa. 59:2</u>
   (Date)

Summarize the Passage_____

_____

How does it apply to my life? _____

Monday _____ Read <u>John 14:6</u>
   (Date)

Summarize the Passage_____

_____

How does it apply to my life? _____

Tuesday _____ Read <u>John 3:16; 1 Tim. 2:5; 2 Cor. 5:21</u>
   (Date)

Summarize the Passage_____

_____

How does it apply to my life? _____

Wednesday _____ Read <u>Titus 3:4-7</u>
   (Date)

Summarize the Passage_____

_____

How does it apply to my life? _____

Thursday _____ Read <u>Rom. 5:8; 1 Peter 3:18a</u>
   (Date)

Summarize the Passage_____

_____

How does it apply to my life? _____

Friday _____ Read <u>Rev. 3:20; John 1:12</u>
   (Date)

Summarize the Passage_____

_____

How does it apply to my life? _____

Saturday _____ Read <u>Rom. 10:9-10</u>
   (Date)

Summarize the Passage_____

_____

How does it apply to my life? _____

Salvation

Friends

Making and hanging around the right kind of friends is one of the most important things you can do as a Christian teenager. The people you hang around with are the ones who usually influence you the most. Teens always list peer-pressure as one of the top two reasons they first tried smoking, drinking, drugs or having sex. When giving an excuse for doing these things, they say, "everybody is doing it." The fact is not everybody is doing it — the people they choose to hang around with, their friends, are the ones doing this. What does the Bible say about making friends? What qualities should you look for?

The Scriptures give us many examples of good friendships. It shows us the friendships of David and Jonathan, Moses and Aaron, Paul and Barnabus, and Jesus and His Disciples to name a few. Scripture also gives us characteristics of good friends. Many of these characteristics are found in the book of Proverbs.

Proverbs 27:17 says, "Iron sharpeneth iron; so a man sharpeneth the countenance of his friend." In other words your friends influence the way you act and look and think just as you influence them in the same manner. Are your friends influencing you in the way of Christ or are they influencing you in the way of sin?

When I was in high school I hung around a group of guys that had bad tempers. Although I didn't have a problem with my temper before I met them, I did shortly after I started hanging around them. Having a bad temper became such a habit with me that even after I quit hanging around those guys and wanted my bad temper to stop, it took many years to get it under control. My friends influenced me to have a bad temper.

At the same time, other friends influenced me to have daily devotions, to pray, to read good Christian books, to reject alcohol, drugs and fornication. Those habits have stayed with me all of my life. I am thankful for that influence in my life.

Friends can influence for good and bad. This week as you look for qualities of friendship in your devotions, analyze your friends: are they influencing you for good or bad? Also analyze yourself: am I influencing my friends for good or bad? What are you going to do about it?

Sunday _____ Read _Prov. 27:17_____
  (Date)
Summarize the Passage_____
_____
How does it apply to my life? _____

Monday _____ Read _Prov. 17:17_____
  (Date)
Summarize the Passage_____
_____
How does it apply to my life? _____

Tuesday _____ Read _James 4:4_____
  (Date)
Summarize the Passage_____
_____
How does it apply to my life? _____

Wednesday_____ Read _1 Sam. 18:1-3_____
  (Date)
Summarize the Passage_____
_____
How does it apply to my life? _____

Thursday _____ Read _Phil. 2:19-22_____
  (Date)
Summarize the Passage_____
_____
How does it apply to my life? _____

Friday_____ Read _Prov. 18:24_____
  (Date)
Summarize the Passage_____
_____
How does it apply to my life? _____

Saturday_____ Read _John 15:12-17_____
  (Date)
Summarize the Passage_____
_____
How does it apply to my life? _____

Friends

Love

Our society has many interpretations of love. In songs we have interpreted love as being a rose and a many splendored thing. In movies and society we see love in the context of lust and sex. Depending upon the family structure we come from, we may see love as expendable in divorce cases and enduring for those who remain married.

You should not be surprised to know that the Bible has a lot to say about love. An entire book in the Old Testament was written about the love of a man for his wife. A chapter in the New Testament was also dedicated to this same subject. In fact, as you read the Bible you will find the subject of love throughout. The Bible could easily be summarized this way: in the Old Testament God showed His love for the Jews/Israel and in the New Testament He showed His love for the world.

As you continue to grow and mature, you must come up with your own definition of love. Those who adopt what movies and society deem as love will have a hard time committing to relationships with friends, with the opposite sex, and with God. Those who seek a biblical definition of love as found in the passages provided this week will build a foundation upon which their future marriage relationships are built, upon which the future relationship with their children is built, and upon which their present and future relationship with God is built.

Before you read the passages provided for you this week I want you to write your definition of love. As you read the Scriptures, compare your definition to what the Bible has to say. Modify your definition each day until you are satisfied that your definition of love is something you want to build the foundation on. Write this definition in the front cover of your Bible and live your life according to that definition. Ten years from now you will be glad you did.

Sunday _____ Read _Gen. 29:9-18_____
            (Date)
Summarize the Passage_____
_____
How does it apply to my life? _____

Monday _____ Read _Gen. 29:19-30_____
            (Date)
Summarize the Passage_____
_____
How does it apply to my life? _____

Tuesday _____ Read _Matt. 22:37-38_____
            (Date)
Summarize the Passage_____
_____
How does it apply to my life? _____

Wednesday _____ Read _Matt. 22:39-40___
              (Date)
Summarize the Passage_____
_____
How does it apply to my life? _____

Thursday _____ Read _1 Cor. 13:1-3_____
             (Date)
Summarize the Passage_____
_____
How does it apply to my life? _____

Friday_____ Read _1 Cor. 13:4-7_____
            (Date)
Summarize the Passage_____
_____
How does it apply to my life? _____

Saturday_____ Read _1 Cor. 13:8-13_____
             (Date)
Summarize the Passage_____
_____
How does it apply to my life? _____

Love

Thou Shalt Not Covet

In English the word *covet* literally means to lust, begrudge or to envy. God tells us not to covet (envy, lust after or begrudge) what other people have.

In our society it is very hard not to covet what other people have. On television we see shows like "Lifestyles of the Rich and Famous," we watch commercials with all of the latest gadgets which are supposed to make our lives more happy. In catalogs, we see models who look fantastic in clothes and we wonder if we would look good in those clothes.

In Colossians 3:5 the apostle Paul calls covetousness idolatry. At first glance it's hard to see the connection between covetousness and idolatry. But look at things from God's point of view: when most people covet after things, they devise plans on how to obtain that possession. Some will work harder and save money to obtain it, some will steal it, still others will belittle and put down others who have what they want. It becomes their focal point on all that they do.

For Christians to covet, we must take our eyes off of God and focus on obtaining the object of our desire. When we take our eyes off of God and focus on obtaining the object, we are no longer relying on God to supply all of our needs because we have set out to work or steal what we believe we need. Also we are no longer relying on God as our source of happiness because we think that this object will fill this void in our lives.

I have seen this many times in Christian service. People desire bigger homes or nicer cars thinking they will bring them more prestige and fulfillment. I know of one man whose one desire is to retire early. He has worked overtime and hoarded his money since he was a child so that he can retire in his 50s. The object of his idolatry – money.

It is impossible to live without wanting and desiring things. The problem comes when we look for these things to make us happy instead of depending on God to fulfill these needs. Are there things in your life that God would consider idols? This week, examine your life and lay these idols at God's feet in prayer. Confess your sin and ask Him to meet this void in your life. Once you ask Him to meet this need – He will!

Sunday _____ Read <u>Col. 3:1-6</u>
               (Date)

Summarize the Passage_____

_____

How does it apply to my life? _____

Monday _____ Read <u>1 Tim. 6:9-11</u>
               (Date)

Summarize the Passage_____

_____

How does it apply to my life? _____

Tuesday _____ Read <u>Hab. 2:9; Eph. 5:5</u>
               (Date)

Summarize the Passage_____

_____

How does it apply to my life? _____

Wednesday_____ Read <u>1 Cor. 6:9-12</u>
               (Date)

Summarize the Passage_____

_____

How does it apply to my life? _____

Thursday _____ Read <u>James 4:1-8</u>
               (Date)

Summarize the Passage_____

_____

How does it apply to my life? _____

Friday_____ Read <u>Ps. 37:3-5</u>
               (Date)

Summarize the Passage_____

_____

How does it apply to my life? _____

Saturday_____ Read <u>Phil. 4:19; Ps. 23</u>
               (Date)

Summarize the Passage_____

_____

How does it apply to my life? _____

Thou Shalt Not Covet

Thou Shalt Not Steal

Looking at the footage of the L.A. riots, supposedly caused by the verdict in the Rodney King beating case, one question has to be asked – is it ever right to steal?

Most people think of someone breaking into a bank or a home, shoplifting, or mugging someone as stealing. The fact is that most stealing in stores is not done by shoplifters but by the employees. A recent edition of "20/20" stated that Americans pay hundreds of dollars extra every year to make up for those who steal.

The word *stealing* covers a whole multitude of sins. The Bible says that not paying tithes is stealing, copying off of someone's paper during a test is stealing, goofing off at work on company time is stealing, and the list goes on. My pastor once brought this point home to me in a sermon when he said even if you take a paper clip that does not belong to you, you are stealing.

Going back to our question – are we ever justified to steal? The answer is *no!* No matter how you have been wronged, no matter how hungry you are, no matter how much you need money, these situations never justify your stealing anything. If you need things you must first pray for your needs, then go to your friends and/or church and ask for help, then take action so that you will not get in the same predicament again.

This week as you read, you will discover many people who thought they could get away with stealing. Take a look at your life. Are you doing anything that would constitute stealing? If so, how are you going to remedy that situation?

Sunday _____ Read Ex. 20:15; Rom. 13:8-14
            (Date)

Summarize the Passage_____

_____

How does it apply to my life? _____

Monday _____ Read Eph. 4:26-28
            (Date)

Summarize the Passage_____

_____

How does it apply to my life? _____

Tuesday _____ Read 1 Cor. 6:9-12
            (Date)

Summarize the Passage_____

_____

How does it apply to my life? _____

Wednesday _____ Read Matt. 6:19-20
            (Date)

Summarize the Passage_____

_____

How does it apply to my life? _____

Thursday _____ Read 2 Peter 4:14-17
            (Date)

Summarize the Passage_____

_____

How does it apply to my life? _____

Friday _____ Read Acts 5:1-11
            (Date)

Summarize the Passage_____

_____

How does it apply to my life? _____

Saturday _____ Read Rom. 2:19-23
            (Date)

Summarize the Passage_____

_____

How does it apply to my life? _____

Thou Shalt Not Steal

Thou Shalt Have No Other Gods

This is an easy commandment for most Christians to *think* they have kept. After all, we don't go to other churches, read other religions' bibles or pray to other religions' gods. We go to a Bible-believing church, read our Bibles, and pray to our God. We have this commandment licked – right?

Wrong! The fact is, in America we worship other types of idols. Some worship movie stars, some rock stars, some sports or athletes, some careers, some education, some cars, some television, some money, some drugs, some alcohol...and the list goes on. If you don't believe me, think back a couple of years ago when many girls dressed just like their idol, Madonna, or think about the recent commercial that kept saying, "I just want to be like Mike" (Michael Jordan). In America, idolatry is marketed to teens. The real tragedy is that teens buy it.

As Christians we are to live in this world but not be of it. In other words, its all right to like basketball, but when your room starts looking like a Chicago Bulls locker room with all the mementos you've purchased and you can recite the statistics of Michael Jordan's basketball career better that you can your Bible verses – you've got a problem and an idol.

See how you do on this idol test:

1. What thing/person/activity do you like more than anything else in the entire world?

2. How much time do you spend thinking about, doing something with or talking about this thing/person/activity?

3. Comparing the time spent on this thing/person/activity to the rest of your day, are you out of balance? Is it taking time that could have been used more effectively?

4. Are you getting complaints from your parents or friends that you are spending too much on this thing/person/activity?

This week as you read the Scripture verses provided, thoughtfully and carefully look around your room, your locker, and your car (if you have one). Do you have anything in your life that is hurting your relationship with others and your walk with Christ? If you do, they are idols. What steps can you take to walk closer with Christ?

Sunday _____ Read _1 Cor. 5:9-13_____
           (Date)
Summarize the Passage_____
_____
How does it apply to my life? _____

Monday _____ Read _1 Cor. 6:9-12_____
           (Date)
Summarize the Passage_____
_____
How does it apply to my life? _____

Tuesday _____ Read _1 Cor. 10:1-15_____
           (Date)
Summarize the Passage_____
_____
How does it apply to my life? _____

Wednesday_____ Read _Eph. 5:1-7_____
           (Date)
Summarize the Passage_____
_____
How does it apply to my life? _____

Thursday _____ Read _Rev. 21:8; 22:14-15_____
           (Date)
Summarize the Passage_____
_____
How does it apply to my life? _____

Friday_____ Read _1 John 5:17-21_____
           (Date)
Summarize the Passage_____
_____
How does it apply to my life? _____

Saturday_____ Read _1 Thess. 1:1-10_____
           (Date)
Summarize the Passage_____
_____
How does it apply to my life? _____

Thou Shalt Have No Other Gods

Thou Shalt Not Take the Name of the Lord Thy God in Vain

Most of us think this is an easy commandment to keep. We do not cuss and we especially don't use God's or Jesus' name in cusswords. We've finally got a commandment that we have not broken – right? While it is true that it is wrong to use God's and Christ's name in cusswords, the real meaning of this commandment goes deeper.

To understand the meaning of this verse we must understand who God is. Our most Holy God knows no beginning and knows no end. He created the world and universe. He created man out of the dust of the earth. He destroyed man when man was rebellious. He gave redemption to man when man didn't deserve it. He loved man so much that He gave His only Son to die on the cross in great pain and humiliation for our sins – what an awesome God.

When we are frivolous in our talk about God we are in essence belittling Him. When we use the phrase "it is the Lord's will" to justify actions that we take or to persuade others, and those actions are not found in Scripture, we have taken the Lord's name in vain.

I remember in school when Christian couples would break up. Usually the one breaking up who has already found someone else to date will say, "It is the Lord's will that we break up." Whether or not it was the Lord's will was not the problem. The problem was that the excuse given to justify breaking up to date someone else was using God's name in vain.

We serve an awesome God, who loves and cares for us. When we frivolously use His name to justify our desires or our actions, we belittle His presence in our lives. As you read this week, take careful note of those who have taken God's name in vain and paid terrible consequences. Are you guilty of taking God's name in vain?

Sunday _____ Read _____
(Date)

Summarize the Passage_____

_____

How does it apply to my life? _____

Monday _____ Read _Matt. 26:69-75_
(Date)

Summarize the Passage_____

_____

How does it apply to my life? _____

Tuesday _____ Read _Ps. 90:2; Hab. 3:6_
(Date)

Summarize the Passage_____

_____

How does it apply to my life? _____

Wednesday_____ Read _Psalm 136_
(Date)

Summarize the Passage_____

_____

How does it apply to my life? _____

Thursday _____ Read _Eph. 4:29-30_
(Date)

Summarize the Passage_____

_____

How does it apply to my life? _____

Friday_____ Read _Col. 3:8-17_
(Date)

Summarize the Passage_____

_____

How does it apply to my life? _____

Saturday_____ Read _Ps. 92:5; 18:30; Heb. 12:29_
(Date)

Summarize the Passage_____

_____

How does it apply to my life? _____

Thou Shalt Not Take the Name of the Lord Thy God in Vain

Does Lying REALLY Hurt?

Lying seems like such a minor sin. We have become so good at it that we don't even realize when we commit "little" lies. Think about the last time someone asked how you were feeling and even though you were not feeling all that well you told them you were feeling fine – you lied. Or consider the last time your parents asked you a question and you only told them half the truth – you lied.

Unfortunately, we live in a society where salesmen who lie get the sales, those who cheat (or lie) on their tests get better grades and those who lie also get elected in the government. If we looked at lying from purely this position we would have to say that lying really does pay off.

But the real facts show that most salesmen who lie are usually found out after the sale is made, those who cheat on their tests usually do poorly on their SATs and in life, and those in government who lie to get elected are usually not reelected and are scorned in the newspapers and media.

There is an immediate payoff for lying, but once you are found to be a liar your reputation is shot and people find it hard to take what you say at face value.

This week as you read the Scripture verses provided, think through the past week. Were there times that you weren't totally honest to your parents, friends or teachers? How do you feel about copying someone else's homework – is that lying? What things should you do to help you be totally honest?

Sunday _____ Read Gen. 12:10-20 _____
　　　　　　　(Date)

Summarize the Passage_____

_____

How does it apply to my life? _____

Monday _____ Read Acts 5:1-11 _____
　　　　　　　(Date)

Summarize the Passage_____

_____

How does it apply to my life? _____

Tuesday _____ Read 1 John 2:18-23 _____
　　　　　　　(Date)

Summarize the Passage_____

_____

How does it apply to my life? _____

Wednesday_____ Read Eph. 4:17-25 _____
　　　　　　　(Date)

Summarize the Passage_____

_____

How does it apply to my life? _____

Thursday _____ Read Col. 3:1-9 _____
　　　　　　　(Date)

Summarize the Passage_____

_____

How does it apply to my life? _____

Friday_____ Read John 8:44; Gen. 3:1-7 ____
　　　　　　　(Date)

Summarize the Passage_____

_____

How does it apply to my life? _____

Saturday_____ Read Prov. 19:5, 9 _____
　　　　　　　(Date)

Summarize the Passage_____

_____

How does it apply to my life? _____

Does Lying Really Hurt?

Hatred = Murder

There is an epidemic of violence in our nation, our schools, and our homes. According to recent statistics, dying from gunshot wounds is the #1 cause of death among black teens and the #3 cause of death among white teens.

I recently talked to a 19-year-old teen who was jailed for burglary, assault, and first-degree murder. He had no remorse for the victims of his crime. He was more concerned about getting himself out of jail. He typifies our world's thinking – he's not sorry for what he did, he's sorry that he was caught.

Most likely you have no thoughts or intentions of ever murdering anyone, but did you know that 1 John 3:15 says, "Whosoever hateth his brother is a murderer: and ye know that no murderer hath eternal life abiding in him."

We must guard our relationships with those we care about and those whom we don't particularly get along with. Remember Christ's plan for resolving conflicts, found in Matthew 18:15-17:

1. Go alone to the person and try to resolve the problem.

2. If the problem is still not resolved, take two or three witness with you to resolve the problem.

3. If you still cannot resolve the problem, ask your youth director if it can be brought up before the youth group.

God's perfect plan for us instead of committing murder or harboring hatred in our heart is found in Romans 12:18, "If it be possible, as much as lieth in you, live peaceably with all men." This week as you read the passages examine your life and relationships. Do you have some unresolved problems that need to be taken care of? What steps are you going to take to resolve those problems?

Sunday _____ Read Matt. 18:15-17 _____
       (Date)

Summarize the Passage_____

_____

How does it apply to my life? _____

Monday _____ Read 1 John 2:9-11 _____
       (Date)

Summarize the Passage_____

_____

How does it apply to my life? _____

Tuesday _____ Read Ex. 20:13; Matt. 5:21-25
       (Date)

Summarize the Passage_____

_____

How does it apply to my life? _____

Wednesday_____ Read Rom. 12:17-21 _____
       (Date)

Summarize the Passage_____

_____

How does it apply to my life? _____

Thursday _____ Read 1 John 3:11-21 _____
       (Date)

Summarize the Passage_____

_____

How does it apply to my life? _____

Friday_____ Read Luke 6:27-35 _____
       (Date)

Summarize the Passage_____

_____

How does it apply to my life? _____

Saturday_____ Read Matt. 5:43-48 _____
       (Date)

Summarize the Passage_____

_____

How does it apply to my life? _____

Hatred = Murder

"Missionary" Dating

A few dedicated teenagers, mostly girls, consider themselves "dating missionaries." A dating missionary dates unsaved or worldly people in order to bring them closer to Christ. Unfortunately for the dating missionaries these relationships are forbidden in the Bible and 99 percent of the cases end tragically for the missionary.

Lets be honest with each other – there is no such thing as a dating missionary. But I have seen many Christian young people get caught up in a relationship with an unsaved person and justify it by saying that they are being a witness to them. Unfortunately, these well-meaning, unsuspecting dating missionaries almost always end up leaving the church, becoming pregnant or marrying into this biblically forbidden marriage.

Look around your church. Notice those who are divorced, those who are single parents, those who attend church while their spouse is at home in bed. Do you think these people thought they would be in this position when they were teens? Of course not. The fact is that some of these people violated God's Word found in 2 Corinthians 6:14, "Be ye not unequally yoked together with unbelievers: for what fellowship hath righteousness with unrighteousness? and what communion hath light with darkness?" They are now paying the price for that disobedience.

A wise Sunday School teacher once told me, "Every date is a future mate." I didn't quite agree with her until I personally saw the tragedies relationships like this usually causes. As you read the passages this week, think about your relationships. Are you dating an unsaved or backslidden person? Do you believe you can contradict what God's Word says without suffering the consequences? Also consider your friendships, are your friends hurting your relationship with Christ? What are you going to do about it?

Sunday _____ Read _2 Cor. 6:14-18_____
            (Date)

Summarize the Passage_____

_____

How does it apply to my life? _____

Monday _____ Read _Gen. 24:1-4; Ezra 9:1-2_
            (Date)

Summarize the Passage_____

_____

How does it apply to my life? _____

Tuesday _____ Read _Deut. 7:1-4_____
          (Date)

Summarize the Passage_____

_____

How does it apply to my life? _____

Wednesday_____ Read _Eph. 5:1-7_____
            (Date)

Summarize the Passage_____

_____

How does it apply to my life? _____

Thursday _____ Read _Eph. 5:8-17_____
          (Date)

Summarize the Passage_____

_____

How does it apply to my life? _____

Friday_____ Read _Eph. 5:21-33_____
        (Date)

Summarize the Passage_____

_____

How does it apply to my life? _____

Saturday_____ Read _James 4:1-10_____
        (Date)

Summarize the Passage_____

_____

How does it apply to my life? _____

"Missionary" Dating

Life and Death

Death is a natural part of life yet it is probably the most misunderstood aspect of our existence. As Christians we interpret death as the beginning of eternal life with Christ for those who believe as we do and the beginning of eternal punishment in hell for those who don't.

Somehow we believe that we are entitled to live a long life. People tend to curse God when a child dies or a seemingly good person is stricken with a dreaded disease while a seemingly bad person lives a long healthy life. Actually, when Christians die, they cross over into the realm of immortal life in heaven. They are "absent from the body and present with the Lord." So when we grieve it is really for our own loss, not for our loved one.

James 4:14 compares our life to a vapor that appears for a little time but quickly vanishes away. This is a beautiful illustration of our existence on earth. If we somehow live 100 years, how does it compare to the thousands of years this world has been in existence. The fact is – it does not. Our lives are just like a vapor when compared to eternity.

The real question is not if we are going to die, it's what are you going to do with the life you have? The fact is that the majority of today's "spiritual giants" (Billy Graham, James Dobson, Jerry Falwell ...) are getting up in age and will eventually die. Who will take their place?

When a tag team wrestler tires, he tags his teammate who steps in to continue the wrestling match. The fact is that the Christian life is a little like the tag team wrestlers. God's plan for Christians is simple – we are to advance His kingdom through evangelism and discipleship. When spiritual giants die their work needs to continue. Are you willing to take their place?

This week as you read the passages provided, look at the people God chose to take the place of the spiritual giants in the past. God chose those who were already spiritually and educationally qualified to take that leader's place. What things can you do to get ready to be used by God? Are there things in your life that would hinder you from being used?

Sunday _____ Read <u>James 4:13-15</u>
       (Date)

Summarize the Passage_____

_____

How does it apply to my life? _____

Monday _____ Read <u>2 Tim. 2:15; Acts 7:20-22</u>
        (Date)

Summarize the Passage_____

_____

How does it apply to my life? _____

Tuesday _____ Read <u>Dan. 1:1-8</u>
         (Date)

Summarize the Passage_____

_____

How does it apply to my life? _____

Wednesday_____ Read <u>Acts 22:3; 9:18-22</u>
           (Date)

Summarize the Passage_____

_____

How does it apply to my life? _____

Thursday _____ Read <u>Luke 2:41-52</u>
          (Date)

Summarize the Passage_____

_____

How does it apply to my life? _____

Friday_____ Read <u>Josh. 1:8-9</u>
        (Date)

Summarize the Passage_____

_____

How does it apply to my life? _____

Saturday_____ Read <u>1 Sam. 16:1, 11-13; 17:40-50</u>
          (Date)

Summarize the Passage_____

_____

How does it apply to my life? _____

Independent but under Authority

Teens often feel that authority is all around them. They have to listen to their parents, to their youth pastors, to their teachers, to their coaches, to police officers, etc. As teens strive for independence and for individuality, a rebellious spirit or attitude emerges in most teens that often drives a wedge between them and the authority figures in their lives.

This is similar to what happened to the prodigal son in Luke 15:11-32. The son went to his father and wanted his inheritance so that he could leave the farm and go to the city and party. What the son found out was that the friends he had when he had money were no longer there when he didn't have anymore. After the money and the friends were gone his partying turned into feeding pigs for a living. Not only did he have to feed them, he had to eat with the pigs. After realizing that his father treated his servants better than he was being treated, he went back home and asked for forgiveness.

Like the prodigal son, most teens do not realize that they are making choices now that they may have to live with the rest of their lives. You may party now, but after the partying, where will you be? Look around you and you will see people living with the choices they made as a teen. You see alcoholics, drug addicts, unwed mothers and fathers, etc. A few years ago they were in your shoes, only they made the wrong choices – what choice are you going to make?

Many parents interpret their teenager's independent spirit as rebellion against the rules and lifestyle that they have set for their household. Unfortunately many teens say and do things at this time in their lives that may never be forgiven or forgotten by their parents.

Someone once said, "The older I get the smarter my father gets." What this guy was saying is that his father was wiser than he ever gave him credit for but he was not smart enough to realize it. Remember your parents are not perfect. They may set guidelines because they have a different view of what is happening than you do and many times they are trying to curb attitudes and habits that may cause you harm in the future.

This week as you read the passages provided, look for areas of conflict between your parents and yourself. What could you do to ease this conflict? In your quest for independence have you hurt others? If so, you need to follow the example of the prodigal son and go back and ask for forgiveness.

Sunday _____ Read <u>Eph. 6:1-2, 5-8</u>
(Date)

Summarize the Passage_____

_____

How does it apply to my life? _____

Monday _____ Read <u>Heb. 13:7, 17</u>
(Date)

Summarize the Passage_____

_____

How does it apply to my life? _____

Tuesday _____ Read <u>1 Tim. 6:1-6</u>
(Date)

Summarize the Passage_____

_____

How does it apply to my life? _____

Wednesday _____ Read <u>1 Peter 2:13-20</u>
(Date)

Summarize the Passage_____

_____

How does it apply to my life? _____

Thursday _____ Read <u>Luke 15:11-32</u>
(Date)

Summarize the Passage_____

_____

How does it apply to my life? _____

Friday _____ Read <u>Titus 2:9-15</u>
(Date)

Summarize the Passage_____

_____

How does it apply to my life? _____

Saturday _____ Read <u>Phil. 2:12-16</u>
(Date)

Summarize the Passage_____

_____

How does it apply to my life? _____

Independent but under Authority

Abortion

No other cause has united America's churches more in the later part of this century than abortion. Since Roe v. Wade was passed, legalizing abortion in the early 1970s, millions of babies have been killed in the name of convenience and birth control.

The sad fact is that Christian girls get abortions every day. Christians have somehow bought into a philosophy that it is all right to cover up one sin by committing another.

Having read extensively on this subject and counseled girls facing this choice, I have noticed three basic excuses that are usually made: 1) if people find out I'm pregnant it will ruin my reputation/testimony; 2) if my parents find out they will kill me or it will ruin their reputation in the church; 3) I can't financially support a baby.

When each excuse is analyzed we see that the girl is actually thinking more about herself than the baby she is carrying. With each selfish excuse she makes, she is denying the power of God in her life to work through the sin she has created.

Young Christian man -- if you fall into sin and your girlfriend becomes pregnant, you are also responsible for what is done to that baby. If that baby is aborted, you are equally responsible for that baby's death.

Christian adoption agencies are always a good alternative to abortion. Did you know that good couples wait years to adopt babies – yet we abort them every day.

Many agencies want to give advice concerning the pregnancy, but take my advice and talk to your parents and youth pastor. Sure your parents will be upset; sure they will be hurt – that's understandable. If you are afraid to tell your parents alone, ask your youth pastor to go with you. It may ease the tension in the room.

This week as you read the passages provided, I want you to think about how God chose men still in their mother's womb to serve Him. I want each of you to determine in your heart that you will not fall into a sexual sin. I want each of you to determine in your heart that abortion is murder and therefore is sin. Analyze your life – are you in a relationship that might lead to sexual sin? If so, what are you going to do about it?

Sunday _____ Read _Gen. 25:19-26_____
          (Date)
Summarize the Passage_____
_____
How does it apply to my life? _____

Monday _____ Read _Isa. 44:2, 24_____
          (Date)
Summarize the Passage_____
_____
How does it apply to my life? _____

Tuesday _____ Read _Isa. 49:1-5_____
          (Date)
Summarize the Passage_____
_____
How does it apply to my life? _____

Wednesday_____ Read _Hosea 12:1-5_____
          (Date)
Summarize the Passage_____
_____
How does it apply to my life? _____

Thursday _____ Read _Luke 1:5-15_____
          (Date)
Summarize the Passage_____
_____
How does it apply to my life? _____

Friday_____ Read _Luke 1:26-45_____
          (Date)
Summarize the Passage_____
_____
How does it apply to my life? _____

Saturday_____ Read _Matt. 19:13-15_____
          (Date)
Summarize the Passage_____
_____
How does it apply to my life? _____

Abortion

Reach Out and Invite Someone

"Reach out and touch someone" was a very successful marketing theme for a major long distance phone service. The word "touch" denotes caring or uplifting. The theme could easily be translated, reach out and show someone you care.

This same theme can be applied to Christian outreach. Statistics show that the average Christian knows nine people who either do not know Christ or are saved but do not attend church. Statistics also show that 80 percent of the people who attend church do so at the invitation of a friend or relative.

These statistics have been proven in my life. In the late 1970s Ron Boothe, at my father's workplace, decided to reach out and invite my father to attend church with him. We were the typical lower middle class family with all the typical family struggles and family conflict. My father and I were always at odds. But, because Ron cared enough about my father, we attended that service and became regular attenders at that church. As a result of one man's invitation, our whole family either rededicated their lives to Christ or accepted Him as personal Savior. My father and I who were once at odds were baptized together a few months after first attending church.

Now let's put these two statistics together. If you are the typical Christian you should have anywhere from seven to nine unsaved or unchurched friends and relatives that you care about. Concentrate the majority of your evangelistic efforts into cultivating deeper relationships with these people to help them come to know Christ and attend church. Remember, concentrating your evangelistic efforts on reaching those you care about does not exempt you from the responsibility of reaching others for Christ, but it helps you be most successful in reaching others for Christ.

This week as you read the passages provided, note the creative ways others reached the lost for Christ. Also this week write down the name of the nine people you will concentrate on reaching. Make a commitment to pray for them every day. Think of different ways to strengthen your relationships. Decide what ways you will present the Gospel to them.

Sunday _____ Read _Luke 19:1-10_____
             (Date)

Summarize the Passage_____

_____

How does it apply to my life? _____

Monday _____ Read _Luke 10:1-12_____
             (Date)

Summarize the Passage_____

_____

How does it apply to my life? _____

Tuesday _____ Read _John 4:6-26_____
             (Date)

Summarize the Passage_____

_____

How does it apply to my life? _____

Wednesday _____ Read _John 4:27-39____
             (Date)

Summarize the Passage_____

_____

How does it apply to my life? _____

Thursday _____ Read _Matt. 28:19-20___
             (Date)

Summarize the Passage_____

_____

How does it apply to my life? _____

Friday _____ Read _Acts 2:14-21, 37-41_
             (Date)

Summarize the Passage_____

_____

How does it apply to my life? _____

Saturday _____ Read _Acts 13:1-2, 44-49_
             (Date)

Summarize the Passage_____

_____

How does it apply to my life? _____

Reach Out and Invite Someone

Just Give Me Some Rock and Roll Music

Music sure has changed in the last 40 years. It has evolved from simple rock and roll as sung by Elvis and Buddy Holly, to the British invasion known most notably by the Beatles and the Rolling Stones, to Acid Rock as sung by Jimmy Hendricks and Black Sabbath, to Disco as sung by the Bee Gee's and Donna Summer, and to Rap Music as sung by M.C. Hammer and 2 Live Crew, Alternative Music as sung by Pearl Jam, and Heavy Metal as sung by Megadeath. As often occurs, lately there's been a resurgence of the old Acid Rock and Disco music. It is hard to tell how music will progress in the future.

One thing is for sure, the message of the music has not changed. From its very conception, rock music has been predicated upon three basic themes: sex, rebellion, and drugs. In fact, the name Rock and Roll was gutter slang for back seat sex. As music styles change, the basic themes they push also change. In the fifties it was rebellion and sex; in the sixties it was rebellion, sex, and drugs; in the seventies it was sex and drugs; in the eighties it was sex; and in the nineties it looks like a resurgence of the sixties themes of sex, drugs, and rebellion, *plus* violence.

You are probably thinking, "Oh no, not another lecture about rock and rap music!" No, I'm not going to lecture you about music. Instead I'm going to let you do the investigating. I want you to write the words to three of your favorite songs. These songs can be Christian, country, rock, rap or anything that you are really into at this moment. After you have written out the songs, compare the lyrics to what the passages provided in your devotions have to say.

As you compare your music to what Scripture says, ask yourself several things:

1. Does the music I listen to glorify God?

2. Does the music promote acts Scripture deems inappropriate?

3. Does this music hinder my walk with Christ and/or my testimony to my unsaved friends?

If your music hinders your walk with Christ, what are you going to do about it? What other types of music should you listen to? What should you do with all those old CDs, tapes and records? As always, this is a decision you have to make. What or who are you going to listen to?

Sunday _____ Read <u>Col. 3:15-17</u> _____
               (Date)
Summarize the Passage_____
_____
How does it apply to my life? _____

Monday _____ Read <u>Ps. 95:1-6</u> _____
              (Date)
Summarize the Passage_____
_____
How does it apply to my life? _____

Tuesday _____ Read <u>Ps. 105:1-3</u> _____
              (Date)
Summarize the Passage_____
_____
How does it apply to my life? _____

Wednesday_____ Read <u>1 Chron. 16:4-12</u> _____
              (Date)
Summarize the Passage_____
_____
How does it apply to my life? _____

Thursday _____ Read <u>1 Chron. 16:23-36</u> _____
              (Date)
Summarize the Passage_____
_____
How does it apply to my life? _____

Friday_____ Read <u>Eph. 5:19-20</u> _____
            (Date)
Summarize the Passage_____
_____
How does it apply to my life? _____

Saturday_____ Read <u>Ps. 33:1-8</u> _____
            (Date)
Summarize the Passage_____
_____
How does it apply to my life? _____

Thou Shalt Not Commit Adultery

Sex, Drugs, and Rock and Roll was the battle cry for teens in the late sixties and things don't seem like they have changed. Those same teens that attended love-ins and Woodstock are now at CBS, NBC, ABC, Fox, HBO, etc. making decisions that affect the viewing habits of over 250 million people in the United States.

Adultery has three definitions in Scriptures:

1. the act of cheating on your spouse,

2. the act of having intimate relations with another person's spouse,

3. the act of thinking (or lusting) about having intimate relations with someone else's spouse.

If we compare these three definitions with our favorite television shows or movies, we will find that the majority of the programs promote this behavior. If we add the scriptural definitions of fornication, we would be hard pressed to find a program that did not promote this behavior in one form or another.

1. the act of having intimate relations outside of marriage,

2. the act of thinking (or lusting) about having intimate relations with another person who is not married.

The question to ask yourself is: if I am to abstain from fornication and adultery, are some of the shows I watch helping me or hindering me from keeping these commandments? This week as you read the passages provided, compare what you are reading to what you are watching. Do the shows you watch promote adultery and fornication? If yes, what changes in your viewing habits are you going to make?

Sunday _____ Read Ex. 20:14; Matt. 5:27-28, 32
  (Date)

Summarize the Passage_____

_____

How does it apply to my life? _____

Monday _____ Read 1 Thess. 4:1-4
  (Date)

Summarize the Passage_____

_____

How does it apply to my life? _____

Tuesday _____ Read 1 Cor. 5:1-13
  (Date)

Summarize the Passage_____

_____

How does it apply to my life? _____

Wednesday_____ Read 1 Cor. 6:9-12
  (Date)

Summarize the Passage_____

_____

How does it apply to my life? _____

Thursday _____ Read Prov. 2:1-22
  (Date)

Summarize the Passage_____

_____

How does it apply to my life? _____

Friday_____ Read Prov. 7:1-27; Rev. 21:8
  (Date)

Summarize the Passage_____

_____

How does it apply to my life? _____

Saturday_____ Read Col. 3:1-17
  (Date)

Summarize the Passage_____

_____

How does it apply to my life? _____

Thou Shalt Not Commit Adultery

Suicide

According to noted youth evangelist and author Jerry Johnston in his book entitled *Who's Talking*, approximately 500,000 teens attempt suicide each year. Ten percent of boys and 18 percent of girls in America have attempted suicide. Each year over 6,000 of them succeed. What brings these teens to the point that death seems the only solution? What does the Bible have to say about suicide?

Many experts cite different reasons teens attempt suicide. Some include drug and alcohol abuse, some cite music which promotes suicide themes and still others blame it on the disintegration of the American family. Whatever the reason, I realize that 10 percent of the boys and 18 percent of the girls reading this have already or at some time in their teen years will attempt suicide.

The Old Testament tells us about a righteous man named Job. Job was very wealthy, he owned a lot of land, he was married and had lots of children. In just one day God allowed Satan to take away all of Job's money, to kill his children, and to persecute Job with boils and sores all over his body. On top of that his own wife told Job to curse God and kill himself. Yet, Job believed God and praised Him.

What a beautiful real life illustration of a man who lost his family, his wealth, and his health but did not even consider suicide even though he was encouraged to. God recognized Job's faith and blessed his health, made him more prosperous than he was before, and gave him more children.

I don't have to argue that suicide is wrong. I bet that 99.9 percent of those who attempt suicide also believe it is wrong. But the fact remains they still attempt to kill themselves. Let me encourage you to consult your parents, your youth pastor, your teachers or your friends if you have thoughts of suicide.

An antiabortion commercial on television says, "Life – what a beautiful choice." Life is worth living. This week as you read the passages provided, yield your life to Christ. Put Him in control of your future, depend on Him when things get rough, praise Him when things get better. Remember like Job, God has a plan and purpose for your life – don't cheat Him or yourself by cutting your life short.

Sunday _____ Read <u>Ex. 20:13</u> _____
            (Date)

Summarize the Passage_____

_____

How does it apply to my life? _____

Monday _____ Read <u>Gen. 37:3-4, 20-36</u> _____
             (Date)

Summarize the Passage_____

_____

How does it apply to my life? _____

Tuesday _____ Read <u>Gen. 39:1-23</u> _____
             (Date)

Summarize the Passage_____

_____

How does it apply to my life? _____

Wednesday _____ Read <u>Gen. 41:14-44</u> _____
               (Date)

Summarize the Passage_____

_____

How does it apply to my life? _____

Thursday _____ Read <u>Job 1:1-22</u> _____
              (Date)

Summarize the Passage_____

_____

How does it apply to my life? _____

Friday _____ Read <u>Job 42:1-17</u> _____
            (Date)

Summarize the Passage_____

_____

How does it apply to my life? _____

Saturday _____ Read <u>Jonah 1,2,3</u> _____
              (Date)

Summarize the Passage_____

_____

How does it apply to my life? _____

Suicide

Honor Thy Father and Mother

A commandment to honor your parents in today's society almost seems antiquated. We live in an era where teens sue, divorce and some even kill their parents. Television shows usually portray parents as bumbling idiots while the teens are obviously wiser and are made to look better than the parents. The teens on television no longer look and act like Beaver Cleaver but usually argue and fight with their parents. How can you be expected to honor your parents when it's cool to be rebellious? How can you be expected to honor your parents when they just don't understand what you are going through?

At the time this commandment was given, teens could literally be stoned (killed) for disobeying their parents. I guess Mom and Dad didn't get much back talk when they asked their kids to clean their rooms!

The fact is that rebellion is not cool. If you looked into the home life of those who look and act rebellious you would find chaos. The fact is that all through life someone has to be in charge. That is the natural order of things. We find this order spelled out in Ephesians where it says the head of wife is the husband, just like Christ is the head of the church. Later in Ephesians it tells the children (teens in your case) to obey their parents in the Lord. In other words there is a chain of command in the family Man ♦ Wife ♦ Teens.

Do your parents know and understand what you are going through? Of course they do. Not that long ago, they were struggling with the same temptations and problems that you do. They set rules and give guidance, based on their wisdom and experience, to help guide you around pitfalls that they foresee coming your way.

Parents are not the bumbling idiots that are portrayed on television. When you are going through tough times, talk to them about it. As you talk, lines of communication will open up between you and your parents. You will discover that they are wiser than you once thought and that it is easier to honor them.

Do you have a tough time honoring your parents? As you read the passages provided, think about how you can open the lines of communication with them. Also write down in the front cover of your Bible the promises that God makes for those who do honor their parents.

Sunday _____ Read _Eph. 6:1-2; Ex 20:12_____
               (Date)

Summarize the Passage_____

_____

How does it apply to my life? _____

Monday _____ Read _Lev. 19:1-3_____
              (Date)

Summarize the Passage_____

_____

How does it apply to my life? _____

Tuesday _____ Read _Deut. 21:18-23_____
             (Date)

Summarize the Passage_____

_____

How does it apply to my life? _____

Wednesday _____ Read _Deut. 5:16_____
              (Date)

Summarize the Passage_____

_____

How does it apply to my life? _____

Thursday _____ Read _2 Tim. 3:1-5_____
             (Date)

Summarize the Passage_____

_____

How does it apply to my life? _____

Friday _____ Read _1 Tim. 5:1-3_____
            (Date)

Summarize the Passage_____

_____

How does it apply to my life? _____

Saturday _____ Read _Col. 3:20; Heb. 12:9____
            (Date)

Summarize the Passage_____

_____

How does it apply to my life? _____

Honor Thy Father and Mother

Temptation

Someone once said I can resist anything except temptation. That statement has some underlying truth. Every one of us has a particular sin that always causes us to stumble. That sin may involve sex, drugs, alcohol, smoking, lying, money, gambling or other vices. Is it wrong to be tempted? Is it wrong to give in?

We have never lived in a time where teenagers have been so bombarded with overt temptations. Commercials, music, sports, movies, and magazines are used by the media to tempt us to give into adultery, fornication, greed, drinking, covetousness, idols, and so on.

Is it wrong to be tempted. No! The Bible says that Christ was tempted far beyond anything we have had to endure, yet he did not give in. But it is wrong to put yourself in the place of temptation. If your particular sin happens to be alcohol, you should not go to places (like some parties) that would put you in a position to sin.

Is it wrong to give in? Of course it is! We have all been in a position where temptation was almost unbearable and we were forced to make a conscious choice of giving in or resisting. The fact remains, whether we gave in or resisted, God's Word is still true – sin is sin and it will always be sin whether we give in or not.

Genesis 39:7-23 tells the story of Joseph who ran from Potiphar's wife when she made sexual advances toward him. Because he ran, and through the lies that Potiphar's wife spread, Joseph was thrown into prison. But God blessed Joseph because of his faithfulness. He was eventually released and given one of the highest ranking jobs in all of Egypt. If you were in that position, would you have run or would you have given in?

What sin or sins tempt you most? Are you purposely putting yourself in areas that cause you to be tempted? This week as you read the passages provided for you, note the times, places, and people that cause you the most temptation. What can you do to avoid these things?

Sunday _____ Read _Gen. 39:7-23_____
              (Date)

Summarize the Passage_____

_____

How does it apply to my life? _____

Monday _____ Read _Matt. 4:1-11_____
            (Date)

Summarize the Passage_____

_____

How does it apply to my life? _____

Tuesday _____ Read _Gen. 3:1-19_____
           (Date)

Summarize the Passage_____

_____

How does it apply to my life? _____

Wednesday_____ Read _Luke 22:39-46_____
           (Date)

Summarize the Passage_____

_____

How does it apply to my life? _____

Thursday _____ Read _James 4:1-10_____
           (Date)

Summarize the Passage_____

_____

How does it apply to my life? _____

Friday_____ Read _James 1:13-15_____
           (Date)

Summarize the Passage_____

_____

How does it apply to my life? _____

Saturday_____ Read _2 Peter 2:1-9_____
           (Date)

Summarize the Passage_____

_____

How does it apply to my life? _____

Temptation

Guys: What to Look for In a Christian Girl

Guys, this week's devotional is meant to give you some practical advice for discovering the qualities of a good Christian wife. Girls, you need to take this week's devotional and apply the characteristics of a good wife to your life.

I learned a very important principle to finding the right wife for my life from a missionary's wife in Guatemala. She said that at the age of 13 she started praying for her future husband. Even though she didn't know him, she prayed that God would mold him into a man of God, would protect him from sins of this world, and that she would know who he was when he came along. I never heard anything like this before so I started the habit of praying for my future wife. Although I dated many girls and was even engaged to be married to someone else, God saved my wife and me for each other. She is the perfect wife for me and I think I'm the perfect man for her. God answers prayer!

Now that you are praying, what qualities should you look for in a woman? First and foremost — your future wife should know Christ and be faithfully serving Him. Too many times people fall in love with someone and as an afterthought they ask the person if she (or he) is a Christian. Many people think their future spouses are Christians but after they get married, find that they are not. Look for someone who is in church and faithfully serving Christ.

Other spiritual qualities are found in Proverbs 31. This chapter gives a beautiful definition of a godly woman. You will discover these qualities as you study your devotions this week.

The other qualities to look for are physical. I'm not talking about physical beauty (although the girl should be attractive to you) but about the other things around her that make her who she is. You should look at her parents and friends — do you like them? Do you get along with them? These are important factors you need to consider.

Money is the number one source of contention in marriages. How does she handle her money? Does she pay her tithes to the church? Does she pay her bills late? Does she spend her money extravagantly? You should know these things before you get married.

There are many other characteristics you should look for. I'm sure your youth pastor could go further into this subject than what I've provided, so if you have any questions ask him. Remember that every date is a future mate. This week discover God's formula for a godly woman.

Sunday _____ Read Prov. 31:10-12 _____
            (Date)

Summarize the Passage_____

_____

How does it apply to my life? _____

Monday _____ Read Prov. 31:13-19 _____
            (Date)

Summarize the Passage_____

_____

How does it apply to my life? _____

Tuesday _____ Read Prov. 31:20-22 _____
             (Date)

Summarize the Passage_____

_____

How does it apply to my life? _____

Wednesday _____ Read Prov. 31:23-25 _____
               (Date)

Summarize the Passage_____

_____

How does it apply to my life? _____

Thursday _____ Read Prov. 31:26-28 _____
              (Date)

Summarize the Passage_____

_____

How does it apply to my life? _____

Friday _____ Read Prov. 31:29-31 _____
            (Date)

Summarize the Passage_____

_____

How does it apply to my life? _____

Saturday _____ Read Prov. 11:16; 12:4 _____
              (Date)

Summarize the Passage_____

_____

How does it apply to my life? _____

Girls: What to Look for in a Christian Guy

Girls, this week I want you to discover the godly characteristics you deserve to have in a husband. You should look for these characteristics in the guys you date and of course in the guy you marry. Guys, you should look at these characteristics and apply them to your life. How do you measure up to God's standard for a Christian man?

Not one chapter is dedicated primarily for the godly man like the one dedicated to the Proverbs 31 woman; however, the Bible is filled with examples of godly men. The characteristics that these men showed are the same characteristics you should look for in a man.

Look back to last week's devotional about praying about your future spouse. Make this a habit in your prayer life. God will guide and direct you as you seek His will for you in a godly husband. The following are other things you should take into consideration:

1. The man should be a Christian and faithfully serving Christ *before* you start dating him. God's Word is very clear about not being unequally yoked with unbelievers.

2. Look for a man who treats his mother well. A man who treats his mother well is prone to treat his wife well. Those who don't treat their mother well tend to treat all women bad.

3. He should handle his money well. Does he save money? What and on whom does he spend his money? Does he tithe? Does he pay his bills on time? Remember money is the number one source of contention in marriages — know his money habits.

4. Be satisfied with the way he is before you get married. Too many girls think they can change a man and make him into what they want. Unfortunately, in 99 percent of the cases that is untrue. Therefore, if he does something that annoys you (drinks, cusses etc.) expect him to do it worse after you are married.

5. What are his goals? If you want to marry a preacher and the guy you date wants to be a businessman or a construction worker — you better think about your priorities and pray about God's will for your life.

6. Do you like his friends and family? These people will play a major role in your relationship with your husband. If you don't like them — it will become a major source of contention between you.

There are many other qualities to look for. Read the passages provided for you and write down those characteristics that you are going to look for in a man, in the front of your Bible.

Sunday _____ Read _1 Sam. 16:12; 17:40-50_
                (Date)

Summarize the Passage_____

_____

How does it apply to my life? _____

Monday _____ Read _Matt. 14:1-4; Mark 6:20_
                (Date)

Summarize the Passage_____

_____

How does it apply to my life? _____

Tuesday _____ Read _Gen. 41:38-41_
                (Date)

Summarize the Passage_____

_____

How does it apply to my life? _____

Wednesday _____ Read _Ps. 1:1-6_
                (Date)

Summarize the Passage_____

_____

How does it apply to my life? _____

Thursday _____ Read _Prov. 1:1-23_
                (Date)

Summarize the Passage_____

_____

How does it apply to my life? _____

Friday _____ Read _1 John 2:12-17_
                (Date)

Summarize the Passage_____

_____

How does it apply to my life? _____

Saturday _____ Read _1 Tim. 6:11-16_
                (Date)

Summarize the Passage_____

_____

How does it apply to my life? _____

The Do's and Don'ts of Dating

Dating is a confusing ritual we go through in our teen years. I'm sure you wish that you could somehow know who the right person is for your life without having to experience the trials and heartache dating causes.

It sure would have been easier if boys were born with a magnet in their head and God's perfect girl for us were born with a piece of metal in her head that would somehow only be attracted to her perfect guy. Imagine the first time they met — talk about being irresistibly drawn together! Unfortunately we are not built this way. Dating is an experience that allows us to evaluate the characteristics in others and how they match up to ways we believe are ideal for us.

When we go through this time of evaluation that we call dating there are certain pitfalls to watch out for – pitfalls that have lured millions of teens into their devastating clutches (pregnancy, venereal diseases, date rape, guilt brought on because of what they've done, etc.). In many cases those teens were never able to fully recover. The following list is in no way meant to be complete, but meant to give you some guidelines for dating:

1. Never, never, never date an unsaved person or someone who is not currently serving the Lord.

2. Never put yourself or your date in a place of temptation. Stay away from a parked car, being home alone or anything or anyplace that might cause you to do something that you know God doesn't want you to do.

3. Watch the physical contact. There is a natural progression to physical relationships. Holding hands leads to hugging and kissing, which may lead to petting, which will in most cases lead to sex.

4. Always listen to your parents. Obey the guidelines that both sets of parents have set. If your date pushes or breaks these guidelines, he or she shows lack of respect for you and your parents.

This week as you study the passages provided, take a sheet of paper and write out a plan of what you would consider to be a perfect date. What activities take place? What do you think should be the motivation/goal behind your date? How does that compare to Scripture?

Sunday _____ Read 2 Cor. 6:11-18
         (Date)

Summarize the Passage_____

_____

How does it apply to my life? _____

Monday _____ Read James 4:1-4
          (Date)

Summarize the Passage_____

_____

How does it apply to my life? _____

Tuesday _____ Read James 4:5-10
           (Date)

Summarize the Passage_____

_____

How does it apply to my life? _____

Wednesday_____ Read 2 Peter 2:1-9
             (Date)

Summarize the Passage_____

_____

How does it apply to my life? _____

Thursday _____ Read 1 Tim. 5:2
            (Date)

Summarize the Passage_____

_____

How does it apply to my life? _____

Friday_____ Read Eph. 6:1-2
          (Date)

Summarize the Passage_____

_____

How does it apply to my life? _____

Saturday_____ Read Matt. 18:20
            (Date)

Summarize the Passage_____

_____

How does it apply to my life? _____

More Do's and Don'ts of Dating

Because of the importance of dating in the lives of teens, this devotional topic has been extended for another week. You may need to review the four guidelines in last week's devotion before you begin.

5. Attend group functions. Double-dating and youth group outings are good, wholesome, and usually economic dates.

6. Never allow yourself to feel pressured into doing something that would cause you to sin. If your date pressures you to do something that you know is wrong — now is the time to break up. The pressure will not stop because you ask him/her to stop — you must put an end to the relationship.

7. Never take verbal or physical abuse from your date. If he or she treats you bad now, it will get worse after you are married.

8. Date people with good Christian reputations. Dating those people also gives you a good reputation and gives you less concern about inappropriate behavior occurring.

9. Pray and dedicate the time you have together, before every date. Asking God to bless your time together will not only get God's blessings on the date but also set the right tone for the evening.

10. Never allow a relationship with someone to take the place of your relationship with Christ.

Last week you wrote out what you would consider to be a perfect date. This week I want you to compare your idea for a perfect date with the dates you presently go on. How do they compare — how do they differ? How do your present dates compare to Scripture? What will you do about it?

Sunday _____ Read 1 Cor. 5:1-8 _____
         (Date)
Summarize the Passage_____
_____
How does it apply to my life? _____

Monday _____ Read 1 Cor. 5:9-13 _____
          (Date)
Summarize the Passage_____
_____
How does it apply to my life? _____

Tuesday _____ Read 1 Cor. 6:9-12 _____
           (Date)
Summarize the Passage_____
_____
How does it apply to my life? _____

Wednesday_____ Read 1 Cor. 6:13-20 _____
            (Date)
Summarize the Passage_____
_____
How does it apply to my life? _____

Thursday _____ Read 1 Thess. 5:22 _____
            (Date)
Summarize the Passage_____
_____
How does it apply to my life? _____

Friday_____ Read Luke 22:40,46 _____
         (Date)
Summarize the Passage_____
_____
How does it apply to my life? _____

Saturday_____ Read Mark 12:29-30 _____
           (Date)
Summarize the Passage_____
_____
How does it apply to my life? _____

Dress for Success

Dress for success was a popular motto in the workplace in the late 1980s. The basic premise was that if you looked successful you would most likely become successful. This theory may or may not be true in the workplace, but in Christianity I believe how we dress plays an important role in our testimony for Christ.

Many questions come up when we talk about dress for Christians. Should guys have long hair or short? Should girls wear tight, short dresses or wear more conservative dresses? Should guys have their ears pierced? How should girls wear their make-up? The questions are endless. Are there any right or wrong answers to these questions — I'll let you be the judge.

This week as you do your devotions, get a piece of paper and make three columns on the page. In the far left column list all of the latest fashion fads that you are currently into (for example: guys with pierced ears, girls with heavy make-up, baggy clothes, tight skirts, etc.). In the middle column (and I really want you to think about this) write down the real reasons you wear these fashions. As you read the passages this week, look at your dress in light of Scripture — and in the last column, mark down what you believe God would think of your dress.

As you can see, I'm not making any judgment calls on how you dress but I'm leaving it all up to you and God. Are you currently dressing in a way that may cause others to stumble? Is your style of dress pleasing to God? What are you going to do about it?

Latest Fashions	Reasons I Wear These Fashions	What the Bible Says

Sunday _____ Read <u>1 Tim. 2:9-10</u>
(Date)

Summarize the Passage_____

_____

How does it apply to my life? _____

Monday _____ Read <u>1 Peter 3:1-6</u>
(Date)

Summarize the Passage_____

_____

How does it apply to my life? _____

Tuesday _____ Read <u>1 Cor. 11:14-16</u>
(Date)

Summarize the Passage_____

_____

How does it apply to my life? _____

Wednesday_____ Read <u>Deut. 22:5</u>
(Date)

Summarize the Passage_____

_____

How does it apply to my life? _____

Thursday _____ Read <u>1 John 2:15-17</u>
(Date)

Summarize the Passage_____

_____

How does it apply to my life? _____

Friday_____ Read <u>1 Thess. 5:22; James 4:17</u>
(Date)

Summarize the Passage_____

_____

How does it apply to my life? _____

Saturday_____ Read <u>Prov. 31:10-31</u>
(Date)

Summarize the Passage_____

_____

How does it apply to my life? _____

Dress for Success

Money: How Do You Manage It?

Someone once said that everybody has their price. I don't believe that is necessarily true of all people. As we look around our world we see many people who give up high-paying jobs to become missionaries or who give up time and energy to help those less fortunate than themselves. Those people may be the exceptions in a world full of greed. Someone also once said money makes the world go round. If that's true — does money make your world go round?

As Americans we live in prosperity unknown throughout history. Our country's poorest people live better than some countries' richest people. Our society measures its success by the amount of *things* it can acquire. Everyone has probably seen the bumper sticker "Those who die with the most toys win." My question is — wins what?

As Christians we must be careful not to be suckered into this way of thinking. Money does not buy happiness. If it did we would be one of the happiest nations in the world. Instead we are one of the most violent nations in the world.

In the Bible God gives us over 2,000 verses that address the subject of money. This week I will give you several of the passages about money. Examine your personal philosophy regarding money in light of what you read this week. Also write down everything you purchase this week and who you buy it for. The Bible says that where your treasure is (what you do with your money) is where your heart is. Did you give your tithe this week? How much money did you spend on yourself — why? In light of Scripture, what should be your attitude toward money?

If you desire more information concerning money, get a topical Bible and look up all the verses pertaining to money. You may also want to go to your local bookstore and purchase a copy of *Gaining Personal Financial Freedom* by Larry Maxwell to further your study on this important subject.

Sunday _____ Read 1 Tim. 6:6-12
        (Date)

Summarize the Passage_____

_____

How does it apply to my life? _____

Monday _____ Read 1 Tim. 6:13-19
        (Date)

Summarize the Passage_____

_____

How does it apply to my life? _____

Tuesday _____ Read Luke 16:1-13
        (Date)

Summarize the Passage_____

_____

How does it apply to my life? _____

Wednesday_____ Read 2 Cor. 9:6-11
        (Date)

Summarize the Passage_____

_____

How does it apply to my life? _____

Thursday _____ Read Ps. 24:1-2; Rom. 14:8
        (Date)

Summarize the Passage_____

_____

How does it apply to my life? _____

Friday_____ Read Mal. 3:8-10; Prov. 3:9-10
        (Date)

Summarize the Passage_____

_____

How does it apply to my life? _____

Saturday_____ Read Luke 12:16-34
        (Date)

Summarize the Passage_____

_____

How does it apply to my life? _____

Building a Barrier against Sin

How can such a small three-letter word cause us so much harm? From the time that Adam and Eve first disobeyed God thousands of years ago, mankind has suffered the terrible scurge of not being able to overcome sin.

When we watch television or listen to the radio it is not hard to see the blatant sins that plague mankind. We live in one of the most degenerate eras in human history. Never before have we been so surrounded by sin. To illustrate my point, notice the changes in society since the 1950s: music's main topic of love was changed to topics of sex and violence; Playboy magazine and other pornographic books and magazines were first published; drugs became a mainstream issue; videotapes, cable, and satellite dishes bring in filth that would have been banned a few decades earlier; violent crime has rampantly increased; and the list goes on and on.

At the same time we see society going downhill, we also have to recognize as Christians we can also be dragged down with it if we're not careful. It is easy to look around and compare ourselves to those around us and think, I'm not that bad. What most Christians don't realize is that God's standard for measurement is not how we compare to those around us, not how we compare to the society we live in, but how we compare to the standards He set for us in His Word.

Let's face it, none of us are without sin when compared to God's standard. We are born into sin and as Christians we struggle with it all the days of our lives. This week you will discover God's plan for overcoming sin in your life. Write down the verses that help you the most in the front cover of your Bible. Memorize some of them. Refer to those verses when you are tempted to sin. If and when you fail, pray for God's forgiveness and try harder next time.

Sunday _____ Read <u>Ps. 119:9-16</u>
    (Date)

Summarize the Passage_____

_____

How does it apply to my life? _____

Monday _____ Read <u>Rom. 8:1-14</u>
    (Date)

Summarize the Passage_____

_____

How does it apply to my life? _____

Tuesday _____ Read <u>Heb. 12:1-3</u>
    (Date)

Summarize the Passage_____

_____

How does it apply to my life? _____

Wednesday _____ Read <u>Rom. 6:1-13</u>
    (Date)

Summarize the Passage_____

_____

How does it apply to my life? _____

Thursday _____ Read <u>1 John 1:8-10</u>
    (Date)

Summarize the Passage_____

_____

How does it apply to my life? _____

Friday_____ Read <u>1 Peter 4:1-8</u>
    (Date)

Summarize the Passage_____

_____

How does it apply to my life? _____

Saturday_____ Read <u>James 4:1-8</u>
    (Date)

Summarize the Passage_____

_____

How does it apply to my life? _____

Building a Barrier against Sin

Forgiveness

What a wonderful privilege it is when we accept Christ to realize that we have been born into a family filled with so many Christian brothers and sisters. We believe that because we are brothers and sisters in Christ, somehow we should live in peace and harmony. Unfortunately, just like our natural brothers and sisters, we have a tendency to fight and quarrel among ourselves.

I believe as Christians we have perfected the art of fighting and criticizing one another. If you go to your local bookstore you will find rows of books criticizing another brother or sister because someone does not like the way they minister to others. Teens often criticize others because they act, look or think differently than they do, or because they're jealous of them, or because they genuinely have a fault and/or sin of which they are unaware.

God knew that we would have this problem and has provided a plan of confronting others with our differences. Matthew 18:15-17 says (paraphrased):

1. If your brother/sister has hurt you in any way, go to and tell him or her alone. If the person repents, you have gained a good friend.

2. If the person refuses to hear you, take two or three people with you to verify the problem and try to resolve the difference.

3. If the person refuses to hear or acknowledge the problem, take him or her before your youth group and/or youth pastor to resolve the problem.

If these steps are taken you will find that in 95 percent of the cases you will not have to go past step 1. Do you have some unresolved conflicts? Has someone wronged you and it has continued to bother you? Have you wronged someone else? Take the actions listed above to resolve those problems. This week as you study the subject of forgiveness, list some steps of how you can be a more forgiving person.

Sunday _____ Read _Matt. 18:15-17_____
              (Date)

Summarize the Passage_____

_____

How does it apply to my life? _____

Monday _____ Read _Eph. 4:26-32_____
              (Date)

Summarize the Passage_____

_____

How does it apply to my life? _____

Tuesday _____ Read _Matt. 18:21-22_____
              (Date)

Summarize the Passage_____

_____

How does it apply to my life? _____

Wednesday _____ Read _Matt. 18:23-35_____
              (Date)

Summarize the Passage_____

_____

How does it apply to my life? _____

Thursday _____ Read _Luke 17:3-4_____
              (Date)

Summarize the Passage_____

_____

How does it apply to my life? _____

Friday _____ Read _Acts 7:54-60_____
              (Date)

Summarize the Passage_____

_____

How does it apply to my life? _____

Saturday _____ Read _Luke 23:13-38_____
              (Date)

Summarize the Passage_____

_____

How does it apply to my life? _____

Forgiveness

Sons and Daughters of God

Have you ever considered what a privilege it is to know Christ as your personal Savior? At the moment of salvation you are immediately adopted into the family of God. You are a son or daughter of Almighty God.

Dr. Harold Wilmington, in *Wilmington's Complete Guide to Bible Knowledge,* said, "He (Christ) was (and is) the Son of God who became the sinless Son of Man that sinful sons of men might become the sons of God."

Just as those who are born into wealthy families or royalty are entitled to the privileges that their family can afford, as the sons and daughters of Christ we also have privileges that are meant for only us. Some of those privileges are listed for you.

1. *Eternal Salvation:* Once you accept Christ as your personal Savior, your eternal home is secure. You never have to worry about where you will spend eternity – your reservation has already been made.

2. *Complete Access to God:* As a child of God you have complete access to confess your sins, to praise and glorify His name, to ask for your needs, and to pray for the needs of others.

3. *The Holy Spirit:* At the moment of salvation the Holy Spirit of God entered your body, soul, and mind. He is there to guide you, to convict you of sin, to give you your spiritual gift(s), and to confirm your salvation.

4. *You Are a New Person:* The Bible tells you in 2 Corinthians 5:17 that when you are saved you are a new creature: "old things are passed away and behold all things are become new."

This week as you read the passages provided for you, think about the price Christ paid so that you could be a child of God and what a wonderful privilege it is to be a child of God. Have you thanked God lately for your salvation? Have you told God you love Him, today? How can you show God each day that you are proud to be His child and that you love Him?

Sunday _____ Read 2 Cor. 5:14-17 _____
            (Date)

Summarize the Passage_____

_____

How does it apply to my life? _____

Monday _____ Read John 10:25-30 _____
            (Date)

Summarize the Passage_____

_____

How does it apply to my life? _____

Tuesday _____ Read Heb. 4:14-16 _____
            (Date)

Summarize the Passage_____

_____

How does it apply to my life? _____

Wednesday_____ Read Eph. 3:1-12 _____
            (Date)

Summarize the Passage_____

_____

How does it apply to my life? _____

Thursday _____ Read John 14:16-26 _____
            (Date)

Summarize the Passage_____

_____

How does it apply to my life? _____

Friday_____ Read John 16:7-15 _____
            (Date)

Summarize the Passage_____

_____

How does it apply to my life? _____

Saturday_____ Read Eph. 4:17-32 _____
            (Date)

Summarize the Passage_____

_____

How does it apply to my life? _____

Sons and Daughters of God

Drugs and Alcohol

Few teens would argue that drugs and alcohol are plaguing your generation. Drug and alcohol use and abuse among teenagers is higher than any time in our history. Why are so many teens buying into this lifestyle? What should be a Christian teen's response to each?

You have grown up in an era in which drug and alcohol use is glamorized in movies, in music, and on television. Our idols in each of these media have portrayed the usage as somewhat cool and sophisticated and the consequences as something not to be taken seriously. Cheech and Chong became rich making albums and movies glorifying the use of marijuana. Beer companies have strategically positioned their commercials around sporting events where teens are most likely to see them. Beer companies also sponsor race cars, country and rock tours and "spring break" parties. Some of the most humorous commercials on television are about beer. Do you know why the beer companies spend millions of dollars advertising to teens who are not old enough to drink...because:

1. They reason that teens already drink, and since they drink they might as well drink their beer.

2. They know teens are their future business. They want to make sure they position *their* beer in the minds of teens before they are legally able to buy beer.

With all of these high-dollar advertisements promoting the use of each, it's no wonder teens are being suckered into this lifestyle.

As Christians we know what our response should be to drugs and alcohol. We should abstain from using them and not attend parties where drinking and drug abuse is taking place. Alcohol and drugs impair a person's thinking, coordination, testimony, and ability to serve God.

As you read the passages provided this week, you will see people who abused alcohol and paid a terrible price for their sin. Also you will see what the Bible says about drinking. Determine that you will not allow yourself to take drugs and alcohol. Also, if you currently have a problem with either drugs or alcohol, seek Christian counseling to overcome this addiction.

Sunday _____ Read _1 Cor. 6:19-20_____
               (Date)

Summarize the Passage_____

_____

How does it apply to my life? _____

Monday _____ Read _Gen. 9:20-25_____
               (Date)

Summarize the Passage_____

_____

How does it apply to my life? _____

Tuesday _____ Read _Gen. 19:30-38_____
               (Date)

Summarize the Passage_____

_____

How does it apply to my life? _____

Wednesday _____ Read _Prov. 4:17; 20:1____
               (Date)

Summarize the Passage_____

_____

How does it apply to my life? _____

Thursday _____ Read _Prov. 23:21-22, 30-34_
               (Date)

Summarize the Passage_____

_____

How does it apply to my life? _____

Friday _____ Read _Gal. 5:17-24_____
               (Date)

Summarize the Passage_____

_____

How does it apply to my life? _____

Saturday _____ Read _1 Peter 4:1-7_____
               (Date)

Summarize the Passage_____

_____

How does it apply to my life? _____

Drugs and Alcohol

Are We Living in the Last Days?

Every generation since Christ's Ascension into heaven has thought that they were living in the last days. Throughout the ages people have studied prophecy to figure out when the tremendous prophecies of the Bible will take place. We live in an exciting time in history. At no other time have so many prophecies been fulfilled concerning the return of Christ than in the past 45 years. How long do we have? How should we spend the time we have left?

In a Christian high school, a Bible teacher asked one of his more pious students what he would do if he knew the Rapture would take place at 12:05 p.m. tomorrow. The teacher expected to hear some spiritual answer like trying to win his friends to Christ or spend the time in prayer, but the student said that he would climb up the highest mountain and about 12:04 and 55 seconds he would jump off the mountain and get the biggest roller coaster ride in history. That's a true story!

The question is, what would *you* do if you knew Christ were coming back tomorrow? Would you witness to your friends? Would you make sure your life was right with Him before He came back? Would you start doing a lot of good deeds? Would you stop listening to some of the music you listen to? Would you stop watching some of the shows you like to watch? Would you clean up your language?

I'm sure if we all knew for sure that Christ would return tomorrow, we would act and do some things differently. The fact is, we don't know when Christ is coming back. He could come today or next year or in 50 years. In the same manner we don't know if we will die today, next year or in 50 years. If we don't know when Christ is coming back or when we will die, doesn't it make sense that we should start cleaning up our lives now?

This week as you read the recommended passages, write down the things you would change if you knew Christ were coming tomorrow. Determine to clean up your life and live as if He were coming back then. Who knows – you might be right!

Sunday _____ Read 1 Thess. 5:1-12 _____
             (Date)

Summarize the Passage_____

_____

How does it apply to my life? _____

Monday _____ Read Matt. 25:1-13 _____
             (Date)

Summarize the Passage_____

_____

How does it apply to my life? _____

Tuesday _____ Read Matt. 25:14-30 _____
             (Date)

Summarize the Passage_____

_____

How does it apply to my life? _____

Wednesday _____ Read James 4:13-17 _____
             (Date)

Summarize the Passage_____

_____

How does it apply to my life? _____

Thursday _____ Read Matt. 24:4-26 _____
             (Date)

Summarize the Passage_____

_____

How does it apply to my life? _____

Friday _____ Read Matt. 24:27-31 _____
             (Date)

Summarize the Passage_____

_____

How does it apply to my life? _____

Saturday _____ Read Matt. 24:32-51 _____
             (Date)

Summarize the Passage_____

_____

How does it apply to my life? _____

Self-Esteem

To some teenagers the teenage years seem like some kind of cosmic joke. For the first 12 years of our lives we barely even acknowledge that the opposite sex exists, then we hit puberty and all we think about is the opposite sex. This is where the joke comes in. During those 12 years of not caring about the opposite sex you never had a pimple in your life and as soon as you start noticing that special someone – all of a sudden that first pimple appears!

This scenario has been played out in millions of American households. During our teenage years we experience many physical and mental changes that cause many teens to question their looks, to question their popularity, and most of all hurt their self-esteem.

Many teenage girls seek plastic surgery to help cover up some apparent flaw, while some guys take steroids to help build up their muscles and self-esteem. Some teens wear outrageous clothes and hairstyles to get attention. Others seek attention by being in the popular cliques in school or in sports. Still others take drugs, drink beer or even seek love and popularity by having sex. All of these are symptoms of a self-esteem problem.

Too many teens are willing to risk the future by taking drugs, steroids, having sex, etc. for temporal satisfaction. God does not make mistakes. He foreknew what you would look like, He knew what social needs you would have, and He knows what you will be in just a few years if you don't give in to temptation.

This week as you study the passages provided for you, think about areas in your life about which you are insecure. Pray and give those areas over to God, acknowledging His working in your life. Also apply the principles of overcoming self-esteem problems to your life.

Four Ways to Overcome Self-Esteem Problems

1. Remember, God does not make mistakes. Trust Him to make you into the man/woman of God He wants you to be.

2. Stop focusing on yourself and get involved. Get involved in your youth group, get involved in your church, and get involved in your family.

3. Stop focusing on yourself and make friends. Making and having friends is one sure way of beating a self-esteem problem.

4. If you have a particular problem you want to overcome (weight, size, popularity, etc.) don't take dangerous shortcuts to overcome your perceived problems. Ask your parents to help you through these perceived problems.

Sunday _____ Read Prov. 14:20-21; 18:24 _____
(Date)

Summarize the Passage_____

_____

How does it apply to my life? _____

Monday _____ Read Ps. 139:13-16 _____
(Date)

Summarize the Passage_____

_____

How does it apply to my life? _____

Tuesday _____ Read Heb. 10:19-25 _____
(Date)

Summarize the Passage_____

_____

How does it apply to my life? _____

Wednesday_____ Read James 2:14-26 _____
(Date)

Summarize the Passage_____

_____

How does it apply to my life? _____

Thursday _____ Read 1 Peter 5:6-7 _____
(Date)

Summarize the Passage_____

_____

How does it apply to my life? _____

Friday_____ Read 1 Sam. 16:7 _____
(Date)

Summarize the Passage_____

_____

How does it apply to my life? _____

Saturday_____ Read 2 Cor. 12:1-10 _____
(Date)

Summarize the Passage_____

_____

How does it apply to my life? _____

Self-Esteem

A Father to the Fatherless

Television sure has changed in the last 30 years. Families are no longer portrayed with a two kids, a mother who stays at home, and a father who works. Television, most experts say, reflects the image of the family. If that's true, then that's why we see today's television family portrayed as two divorced people (with kids) getting married, two single mothers living together to save on expenses, or a father raising the family alone.

According to Donald Hernandez, chief of the Census Bureau's marriage and family branch, 27 percent of our nation's teens live in a home without a father. The majority of the fatherless homes is due to divorce.

One of the most comforting things for Christian teens who have lost their fathers due to death or divorce should be that you have a father in heaven who loves, cares, and hears your every word and cry. He is there to comfort your hurts, provide for your needs, correct and forgive you when you sin, pick you up when you fall, love you when you are unlovable, direct your path, and bless you far above anything that you could ever ask or think. What a wonderful heavenly Father we have.

Is your heart full of sorrow, bitterness or confusion because your father is no longer with you? Cast all of your cares upon your heavenly Father because He cares for you. You are no longer fatherless, you are no longer alone. God the Father is always with you and has sent the Holy Spirit to comfort you.

In the passages provided, write down characteristics of God the Father inside the cover of your Bible along with the phrase, "I am not alone. I have a Father in heaven who loves, cares, and provides for my every need." If your earthly father still lives with you, thank God for your father and set out to do something extra special for him this week. If you have a stepfather, think about what you can do to build a good relationship with him, and pray for God's help in relating to him.

Sunday _____ Read Luke 11:2-4 _____
              (Date)

Summarize the Passage_____

_____

How does it apply to my life? _____

Monday _____ Read 1 Cor. 8:6; Rom. 8:14-17
              (Date)

Summarize the Passage_____

_____

How does it apply to my life? _____

Tuesday _____ Read Ps. 68:1-5 _____
              (Date)

Summarize the Passage_____

_____

How does it apply to my life? _____

Wednesday _____ Read Ps. 10:1-18 _____
              (Date)

Summarize the Passage_____

_____

How does it apply to my life? _____

Thursday _____ Read Ex. 22:21-24 _____
              (Date)

Summarize the Passage_____

_____

How does it apply to my life? _____

Friday _____ Read Deut. 10:17-21 _____
              (Date)

Summarize the Passage_____

_____

How does it apply to my life? _____

Saturday _____ Read Jer. 32:17-19, 27; Josh. 1:5-6a
              (Date)

Summarize the Passage_____

_____

How does it apply to my life? _____

Mistakes – Starting Over

Jim Dethmer from Willow Creek Community Church once told a story about a 100-yard-dash he read about in the paper. This was no ordinary race, it was the Special Olympics. The race began like all others, with the shot from a gun. All of the contestants started fine, then a few meters down the track one of them fell down. The others ran for a few more meters and then without anyone saying anything they all stopped and went back to help their fellow contestant. They helped him up, dusted him off, then they ran the rest of the race arm in arm.

What a beautiful illustration of the Christian life. Those Special Olympic contestants learned something that most Christians never learn – that is, we're all going to fall, it's just a matter of when and how far. If we know we're going to fall, it behooves us to help others when they fall so that they may help us when we fall.

Have you fallen? Have you been involved in some activity that would displease God? Are you an unwed mother, pregnant, a drug user, a homosexual, or have you just plain turned your back on God? Remember that God has not turned His back on you. Are you going to stay down or are you going to get back into the race?

Someone once said that Christians are the only army who shoot their wounded. So many times we want to give up on those who fall – but God who is full of forgiveness, always forgives when asked. If He can forgive, so can you. Do you know someone who has fallen? Do you know someone who was once on fire for God but now has turned away? Are you going to help them get back into the race?

This week as you read the passages provided, think about you and those around you. Do you need help getting back into the race? Call your youth pastor and ask him for help. Do you know someone who needs help? Go to them and confront them. Ask them how you can help them get back on their feet and into the race.

Sunday _____ Read _Prov. 24:16_____
                    (Date)

Summarize the Passage_____

_____

How does it apply to my life? _____

Monday _____ Read _Matt. 18:21-35_____
                    (Date)

Summarize the Passage_____

_____

How does it apply to my life? _____

Tuesday _____ Read _Luke 17:3-4_____
                    (Date)

Summarize the Passage_____

_____

How does it apply to my life? _____

Wednesday_____ Read _1 Cor. 2:4-11_____
                    (Date)

Summarize the Passage_____

_____

How does it apply to my life? _____

Thursday _____ Read _Col. 3:12-13_____
                    (Date)

Summarize the Passage_____

_____

How does it apply to my life? _____

Friday_____ Read _Gal. 6:1-6_____
                    (Date)

Summarize the Passage_____

_____

How does it apply to my life? _____

Saturday_____ Read _Luke 15:11-24_____
                    (Date)

Summarize the Passage_____

_____

How does it apply to my life? _____

Mistakes - Starting Over

How Do We Love God?

We all know of God's love for us found in John 3:16. Thousands of books and millions of sermons have proclaimed this valuable information of God's love for all people in spite of our sin. Not too many books have been written on how we are to love God back. At Christmas we have all asked, "How do you buy something for someone who has everything?" As Christians we have the same dilemma – how do we love God who is love?

In Matthew 22:37 Jesus said, "Thou shalt love the Lord thy God with all thy heart, and all thy soul, and with all thy mind." Here Christ has given us a guide for loving God. Basically humans are made up of the three areas talked about in this verse.

1. *Heart:* represents the emotional part of our lives. The heart is where our love and compassion for others comes from.

2. *Soul:* represents the spiritual part of our lives. Obviously if we do not love God in our soul, we would not be saved.

3. *Mind:* represents the intellectual part of our lives. Your mind controls the way you think, talk, and act.

The love of God must comprise all of our heart, all of our soul, and all of our mind. In the Old Testament, the Israelites had to make a sin offering to God. In this offering they did not cut up the animal and keep part of it for themselves; they presented the entire animal on the altar.

How do we love God? We show God that we love Him by yielding our entire life to Him. Can we really love God if we have lust in our heart? Can we love God if we have not trusted Christ as our personal Savior? Can we love God if we continue to fill our minds with trash?

This week as you read the suggested passages, consider your love for God. Have you yielded your heart, mind, and soul to Him? Pray and give these areas to God. Also, as God shows His love for you every day by providing your every need, make it a point to tell God you love Him every day.

Sunday _____ Read <u>Matt. 22:36-37</u>
(Date)

Summarize the Passage_____

_____

How does it apply to my life? _____

Monday _____ Read <u>John 8:42; 14:15</u>
(Date)

Summarize the Passage_____

_____

How does it apply to my life? _____

Tuesday _____ Read <u>John 14:21-24</u>
(Date)

Summarize the Passage_____

_____

How does it apply to my life? _____

Wednesday _____ Read <u>1 John 4:17-19</u>
(Date)

Summarize the Passage_____

_____

How does it apply to my life? _____

Thursday _____ Read <u>1 John 5:1-4</u>
(Date)

Summarize the Passage_____

_____

How does it apply to my life? _____

Friday _____ Read <u>Rom. 12:1-2</u>
(Date)

Summarize the Passage_____

_____

How does it apply to my life? _____

Saturday _____ Read <u>1John 2:1-5; John 15:7-14</u>
(Date)

Summarize the Passage_____

_____

How does it apply to my life? _____

Love Your Neighbor as Yourself

Matthew 22:39 gives the second greatest commandment, "And the second is like unto it (last week's devotion), Thou shalt love thy neighbor as thyself." Is our neighbor just next door or has Jesus commanded our love be shown to all men? How can we possibly begin to fulfill such a commandment?

Your neighbors are people you come in contact with every day. Your neighbors include your teachers, your friends, your enemies, your bus driver, your family, and your relatives. You are supposed to love the good and the bad, the old and young, the pretty and ugly.

How do you love someone else like you love yourself? The first thing you need to do is consider everything you do for yourself every day.

1. You feed yourself when you are hungry.

2. You clothe yourself when you are cold.

3. You clean yourself up when you are dirty.

4. You forgive yourself when you do something wrong.

5. You buy yourself things you need.

In other words, you take care of all of your own physical, mental, and spiritual needs every day. When you see your neighbor in need, you should have a natural spiritual reaction to try to help meet that need. When you seek to meet the physical, mental, and spiritual needs of others as you seek to meet those needs in your life, you love others as you love yourself.

Do you know someone who has a need? Do you attempt to meet those needs in others?

This week as you read the passages provided for you, consider this question: Do I really love my neighbors as myself? Begin this week to start meeting the needs of others. You will soon find that the gift of giving to others reaps rewards that only eternity could repay.

Sunday _____ Read Matt. 22:36-40 _____
                    (Date)

Summarize the Passage_____

_____

How does it apply to my life? _____

Monday _____ Read 1 John 4:7-16 _____
                    (Date)

Summarize the Passage_____

_____

How does it apply to my life? _____

Tuesday _____ Read 1 John 4:20-21 _____
                    (Date)

Summarize the Passage_____

_____

How does it apply to my life? _____

Wednesday_____ Read Rom. 12:9-21 _____
                    (Date)

Summarize the Passage_____

_____

How does it apply to my life? _____

Thursday _____ Read John 13:34-35 _____
                    (Date)

Summarize the Passage_____

_____

How does it apply to my life? _____

Friday_____ Read 1 John 3:16-24 _____
                    (Date)

Summarize the Passage_____

_____

How does it apply to my life? _____

Saturday_____ Read Luke 10:30-37 _____
                    (Date)

Summarize the Passage_____

_____

How does it apply to my life? _____

Love Your Neighbor as Yourself

How to Lead Others to Christ

One of the greatest privileges we have as Christians is the ability to share the way of eternal salvation to our lost friends and loved ones. Unfortunately few Christians have ever led someone to Christ because they have never been taught. God commands us to "be ready always to give an answer to every man that asketh you a reason of the hope that is in you with meekness and fear" (1 Peter 3:15). This devotional is dedicated to help you begin to master God's plan of salvation.

Preparation:

A. Write down your personal testimony of how you became a Christian. Don't glorify your past, briefly mention what brought you to the point of salvation, how you got saved, and what your life has been since you became a Christian.

B. Highlight verses in your Bible that pertain to salvation. Some of those verses will be provided for you in the devotional lessons this week.

C. Write down those verses and the page numbers in the front or back cover of your Bible.

D. Memorize those verses and in your own words give the meaning of each verse.

E. Memorize your testimony.

F. Develop a plan you are comfortable with in sharing the Gospel of Christ. This needs to include:

1. Man's sin and inability to save himself: Romans 3:23, Romans 6:23, Isaiah 59:2.

2. God's love for man and the precious gift Christ gave: John 3:16, 1 Timothy 2:5, Romans 5:8, 1 Peter 3:18a.

3. What a person needs to do to be saved: Revelation 3:20, John 1:12, Romans 10:9.

4. How to accept Christ:

   a. Admit that you are a sinner.

   b. Be willing to turn from your sins.

   c. Believe that Christ died for you on the Cross and rose from the grave.

   d. Pray and invite Jesus Christ to come in and control your life through the Holy Spirit.

G. Rehearse, rehearse, rehearse!

Sunday _____ Read _1 Peter 3:15-16_____
                (Date)

Summarize the Passage_____

_____

How does it apply to my life? _____

Monday _____ Read _Matt. 28:19-20_____
                (Date)

Summarize the Passage_____

_____

How does it apply to my life? _____

Tuesday _____ Read _Mark 16:15-16_____
                (Date)

Summarize the Passage_____

_____

How does it apply to my life? _____

Wednesday_____ Read _2 Tim. 2:15-26_____
                (Date)

Summarize the Passage_____

_____

How does it apply to my life? _____

Thursday _____ Read _1 Tim. 2:1-4_____
                (Date)

Summarize the Passage_____

_____

How does it apply to my life? _____

Friday_____ Read _1 Tim. 4:9-12_____
                (Date)

Summarize the Passage_____

_____

How does it apply to my life? _____

Saturday_____ Read _Acts 26:16-18_____
                (Date)

Summarize the Passage_____

_____

How does it apply to my life? _____

How to Lead Others to Christ (Part 2)

How to Witness

Before continuing this series on sharing Christ, write down the teens you know who don't know Christ or who don't attend church. Now list them in priority of those you care about the most. Concentrate on the top seven people on your list. These are the people who will probably be the most receptive to hearing the Gospel or attending church at your request.

A. When sharing Christ with others you must decide the best place and circumstances needed to share this valuable information. The Holy Spirit will direct your thoughts and actions concerning this.

B. Sharing Christ takes time to master. It will take practice and several times of sharing Christ with someone before you start to feel comfortable doing it.

C. Start with something you have in common with that person or address a problem the person may be struggling with. For example, "Tom, I heard you are trying to quit smoking. How's that going?" After that, you are open to share how Christ helped you or someone you know to overcome a bad habit. Depending on Tom's response you may be able to witness to him. If he's not receptive save it for another time.

D. Your witness does not necessarily have to be your verbally sharing Christ with them. You can invite them to church to hear a special speaker or attend a special event, have your youth pastor help you share Christ with them, or share a Gospel tract or audiotape. There are many ways to witness to others.

E. After leading someone to Christ, be sure to get them into church. Introduce them to your Youth Pastor and friends. Ask your youth pastor to help disciple your friend.

This week study the salvation verses provided. What do these verses mean to you? Take the time to thank Christ for the salvation He has provided for you. Decide who you will share Christ with and think of creative ways to do it. Pray for guidance and direction. God will bless your faithfulness.

Sunday _____ Read John 14:6 _____
(Date)

Summarize the Passage_____

_____

How does it apply to my life? _____

Monday _____ Read John 3:16 _____
(Date)

Summarize the Passage_____

_____

How does it apply to my life? _____

Tuesday _____ Read Rom. 3:23; 6:23 _____
(Date)

Summarize the Passage_____

_____

How does it apply to my life? _____

Wednesday_____ Read Isa. 59:2 _____
(Date)

Summarize the Passage_____

_____

How does it apply to my life? _____

Thursday _____ Read John 1:2 _____
(Date)

Summarize the Passage_____

_____

How does it apply to my life? _____

Friday_____ Read 1 Cor. 5:21 _____
(Date)

Summarize the Passage_____

_____

How does it apply to my life? _____

Saturday_____ Read Rev. 3:20; Rom. 10:9 ____
(Date)

Summarize the Passage_____

_____

How does it apply to my life? _____

Why Do the Wicked Prosper?

This question has been asked by just about every person who has ever lived. Sometimes it doesn't make sense when we see a semingly good person struck down with a terrible disease and other seemingly bad people appear to prosper. Why do the Madonnas and the Hugh Hefners of this world seem to thrive and you and I struggle to get enough money to survive? God just doesn't seem fair.

God is not supposed to be "fair." Actually God is more than fair with mankind who is born with a sinful nature in direct opposition to Him. God is perfect, holy, merciful, full of grace and righteousness. Isaiah 64:6 says our good works are as filthy rags in God's sight. Nothing we could ever do could ever earn God's favor. Only by God's grace and mercy are we saved, otherwise we would all deserve to go to hell whether we were "good or bad."

We like to compare ourselves to others to show our righteousness before God. Sure our lives look pretty good when we compare them to Madonna, Hugh Hefner or a death-row murderer, but when compared to God we all deserve the same punishment – hell.

Someone once said, "Earth is the only heaven some people will ever see and it is the only hell Christians will ever see." When you see the unrighteous prosper, think about how God showed His mercy and grace to you when you accepted Christ. God is showing the unrighteous the same mercy He has shown you.

This week instead of hoping for the wicked's demise, pray for their salvation. God who worked the miracle of salvation in our lives can also work that same miracle in theirs.

Sunday _____ Read _Ps. 73:3-28_____
         (Date)

Summarize the Passage_____

_____

How does it apply to my life? _____

Monday _____ Read _Ps. 94:1-23_____
          (Date)

Summarize the Passage_____

_____

How does it apply to my life? _____

Tuesday _____ Read _Prov. 24:1-22_____
           (Date)

Summarize the Passage_____

_____

How does it apply to my life? _____

Wednesday _____ Read _Ps. 58:1-11_____
             (Date)

Summarize the Passage_____

_____

How does it apply to my life? _____

Thursday _____ Read _Prov. 21:10-16_____
            (Date)

Summarize the Passage_____

_____

How does it apply to my life? _____

Friday_____ Read _Ps. 37:1-22_____
         (Date)

Summarize the Passage_____

_____

How does it apply to my life? _____

Saturday_____ Read _Ps. 37:23-40_____
           (Date)

Summarize the Passage_____

_____

How does it apply to my life? _____

Situation Ethics
What's Right and What's Wrong?

Study after study has shown that today's teens and adults don't actually believe that there are moral absolutes by which we are to live. Moral absolutes are the things we believe are right no matter what the circumstances.

Situation ethics believes that the situation determines your action. For example, most people believe sex outside of marriage is wrong, but millions of teens compromise their beliefs when put in this situation and others. They try to rationalize their desires by asking:

1. Are we ever right to have premarital sex because we are in love?

2. Are we ever justified to lie to get a friend or ourselves out of trouble?

3. Are we ever justified to abort a baby because we cannot afford to raise it?

That is situation ethics.

Are we free to pick and choose which commandments we'll keep and which we won't? Of course not! God's Word stands true. We are to obey God's Word – no matter what the circumstance.

See if you pass the situation ethics test:

1. Have you ever lied to get yourself or your friend out of trouble?

2. Have you ever felt justified while cheating on a test?

3. Have you ever done something that you knew was wrong but felt the circumstance warranted the action?

Someone once said that it is never right to do wrong to do right. In other words, the end never justifies the means. You are never right to break a commandment to do what you feel may be right. This week as you study the passages provided, recall instances in the past where you've been guilty of situation ethics. How would you do that differently today?

Sunday _____ Read _Rom. 1:19-32_____
                  (Date)

Summarize the Passage_____

_____

How does it apply to my life? _____

Monday _____ Read _Rom. 6:1-7_____
                  (Date)

Summarize the Passage_____

_____

How does it apply to my life? _____

Tuesday _____ Read _Rom. 6:8-14_____
                  (Date)

Summarize the Passage_____

_____

How does it apply to my life? _____

Wednesday _____ Read _Rom. 6:15-23_____
                  (Date)

Summarize the Passage_____

_____

How does it apply to my life? _____

Thursday _____ Read _Ex. 20:1-17_____
                  (Date)

Summarize the Passage_____

_____

How does it apply to my life? _____

Friday _____ Read _Matt. 22:36-40_____
                  (Date)

Summarize the Passage_____

_____

How does it apply to my life? _____

Saturday _____ Read _James 4:17; Eph. 5:8-17_____
                  (Date)

Summarize the Passage_____

_____

How does it apply to my life? _____

Situation Ethics

Formula for Christian Success

If you really want to know who you are, look at what you are when you are alone. Also, think of what you would do if you could do it. That's the real you. God knows your innermost desires. In other words, the facade that we put on at church or at school doesn't really mean anything to God. What really matters to God is what you are when you are at home, what you do when you are alone, and what thoughts you let occupy your mind.

First Samuel 6:7 says, "...for the Lord seeth not as a man seeth; for man looketh on the outward appearance, but the Lord looketh on the heart." God knows who we are when we're out in public and He knows who we are when we're alone. He knows how we talk when we're out in public and He knows what we think about when we're alone.

The formula listed in this devotional is meant to help you succeed in your Christian life. Too many teens are playing the Christian game and have not really committed their life to Christ. When I first started attending church, I was amazed at how many people whom I thought were my friends attended that church but never reached out and invited me to attend church with them. The teens were playing the game. They went to church on Sunday but lived like they wanted when they were at home.

1. *Know what you believe:* Study God's Word every day, read good Christian books, and pray. If you make this a spiritual habit in your life, you will begin to control your thought life.

2. *Share what you believe:* Don't be afraid to share what God is doing in your life to your unsaved or unchurched friends and family. Share the Gospel with them and invite them to church.

3. *Live what you believe:* Be consistent in your walk with Christ at church and at home, at school and in your youth group, while playing sports or doing your devotions.

When I became a Christian I determined that I was not going to play the game. Without knowing it I applied the formula to my life and had victory over sin, grew much faster in my walk with Christ than my other Christian friends, and have shared my faith with hundreds of others.

Do you want spiritual success in your life? Do you want victory over sin? This week as you read the passages provided, write down a plan of how you will apply this formula to your life.

Sunday _____ Read _Josh. 1:8-9_____
        (Date)

Summarize the Passage_____

_____

How does it apply to my life? _____

Monday _____ Read _2 Tim. 2:15; Matt. 6:32-34_
        (Date)

Summarize the Passage_____

_____

How does it apply to my life? _____

Tuesday _____ Read _Jer. 33:3; Phil. 4:5-7___
        (Date)

Summarize the Passage_____

_____

How does it apply to my life? _____

Wednesday_____ Read _Luke 10:1-2_____
        (Date)

Summarize the Passage_____

_____

How does it apply to my life? _____

Thursday _____ Read _Phil. 3:13-17_____
        (Date)

Summarize the Passage_____

_____

How does it apply to my life? _____

Friday_____ Read _Matt. 5:13-16_____
        (Date)

Summarize the Passage_____

_____

How does it apply to my life? _____

Saturday_____ Read _Phil. 1:20-21_____
        (Date)

Summarize the Passage_____

_____

How does it apply to my life? _____

Prayer

What would you say to the President of the United States if you had the opportunity? Would you talk about world affairs, poverty, health reform, education reform, the prolife movement or even religious freedom? We live in a nation of over 250,000,000 Americans and sadly less than one percent of those people will ever have the chance to sit down and talk to the President.

What will you say to God when you get to heaven. Will you ask Him questions about why certain things happened here on earth? Will you confess sins that you harbored in your heart or will you just praise Him for who He is?

What a privilege we have to be able to talk to God at anytime or anyplace. We do not have to wait to get to heaven to praise Him, to confess our sins or to ask Him why certain things happen to us here on earth. God has provided this access to Him through prayer.

Some teens ask why it is necessary to pray – after all God knows our needs before we even ask them. In a nutshell we pray for three reasons:

1. God tells us to pray – Colossians 4:2

2. Christ prayed – Luke 6:12-16

3. God answers prayer – Matthew 21:22

A simple pattern for prayer is found in the acronym A.C.T.S.

Adoration: Adoring or praising God for who He is.

Confession: Confessing to God those sins we have committed today. You should confess your sins every day.

Thanksgiving: Thanking God for forgiveness of your sins, for salvation, for what He has done in your life, and what He is currently doing in your life.

Supplication: A) Petition: asking God to meet your needs.
B) Intercession: asking God to meet others' needs.

Remember that prayer is simply talking to God. This week as you read about prayer in your devotions, make prayer a habit in your life. Utilize the ACTS pattern for prayer. Keep a log of your requests and the answers to your prayers.

Sunday _____ Read Col. 4:2; Matt. 21:22 _____
           (Date)

Summarize the Passage_____

_____

How does it apply to my life? _____

Monday _____ Read Luke 6:12-16 _____
           (Date)

Summarize the Passage_____

_____

How does it apply to my life? _____

Tuesday _____ Read Jer. 33:3 _____
           (Date)

Summarize the Passage_____

_____

How does it apply to my life? _____

Wednesday _____ Read James 5:15-16 _____
           (Date)

Summarize the Passage_____

_____

How does it apply to my life? _____

Thursday _____ Read Heb. 4:14-16 _____
           (Date)

Summarize the Passage_____

_____

How does it apply to my life? _____

Friday_____ Read John 14:12-15 _____
           (Date)

Summarize the Passage_____

_____

How does it apply to my life? _____

Saturday_____ Read 2 John 5:11-15 _____
           (Date)

Summarize the Passage_____

_____

How does it apply to my life? _____

Prayer

Balancing Your Life

Have you been in a car that had an out-of-balance front end? The front end seems to shake, the car is harder to drive, and the tires wear out faster. Most Christians do not realize that God wants us to live a balanced life. If we become unbalanced in our walk with Christ we can suffer similar consequences as the car.

What is a balanced life? The balanced life is made up of four areas: physical, mental, spiritual, and social. If we effectively master three of these areas and not the other we become unbalanced which makes us a less effective person and servant of Christ. Let's define each of these areas (two this week and two next week):

1. *Physical:* Physical takes in the physical shape of your body, the amount of sleep you get, the kind of food you eat, the work you do, etc.

If your physical shape is in poor condition, it hampers the Spirit's work through your life. Being in poor physical shape can cause high blood pressure, increased weight, heart problems, and even an early death.

The abuse of overexercising can be as mentally and spiritually damaging to yourself as not excercising at all. Too many Christians have bought into this body building movement. It shouldn't be called body building but body worshipping, because people spend more time in front of a mirror looking at themselves than looking toward God. Many have a tendency to be more violent in their behavior, begin to commit idolatry (by worshipping themselves) and vanity. Be careful not to fall into this trap. What kind of shape are you in? Are you spending *too much* time working out or *not enough* time?

2. *Mental:* The mental part of this balance has to do with education, reading, etc. The mental is important because, in today's world, if you are ever going to do anything for God, you need to hit the books. Graduating from high school and college is important. Having your daily devotions and reading godly books to stimulate your spiritual growth is also important. Those who have the discipline to study while they are young will most likely still be used of God when they are old.

The abuse of over-education: Too many people believe education is an end in itself. They are in constant pursuit of more and more knowledge and unfortunately cannot adequately communicate with others. Because of overzealous pursuit of knowledge they tend to emphasize physical exercise thus making their lives out of balance.

(See next week's devotion for more on "Balancing Your Life.")

Sunday _____ Read _1 Tim. 4:7-8_____
               (Date)

Summarize the Passage_____

_____

How does it apply to my life? _____

Monday _____ Read _Col. 2:20-23_____
               (Date)

Summarize the Passage_____

_____

How does it apply to my life? _____

Tuesday _____ Read _1 John 2:15-17_____
               (Date)

Summarize the Passage_____

_____

How does it apply to my life? _____

Wednesday_____ Read _1 Sam. 16:12; 17:42____
               (Date)

Summarize the Passage_____

_____

How does it apply to my life? _____

Thursday _____ Read _2 Tim. 3:1-7_____
               (Date)

Summarize the Passage_____

_____

How does it apply to my life? _____

Friday_____ Read _2 Tim. 3:14-17_____
               (Date)

Summarize the Passage_____

_____

How does it apply to my life? _____

Saturday_____ Read _Ps. 119:9-16, 33-40____
               (Date)

Summarize the Passage_____

_____

How does it apply to my life? _____

Balancing Your Life (Part 2)

This week we will examine two other areas essential to a balanced life.

3. *Social:* This area surprises most Christians because they think it is a sin to enjoy themselves. God made us social beings. One of the main functions of the church is for Christian fellowship. There is nothing wrong with pursuing fun activities and enjoying our brothers and sisters in Christ.

The abuse of not having a social life tends to affect our mental thinking. I remember when I was a teen, I worked my way though a Christian High School by cleaning the building several hours a night. On top of that I had to keep up with my studies, attend church three times a week, go on Thursday-night visitation, go to teen club on Saturday night, and work all weekend at the church. I had no time for the social part of my life – I was out of balance. Because of lack of adequate sleep I had a short temper, and I generally became a miserable person. When my youth pastor pointed out that I was out of balance, I was able to schedule time for my social activities and sleep.

The other extreme is those who pursue too much social activity. These people tend to want to come to the social activities at the church but not to the spiritual activities. They often lack true spiritual depth. Are you socially balanced?

4. *Spiritual:* Most people don't realize that this area of our lives also needs to be balanced. If we neglect this area we are prone to commit more sin, to lack the power of God in our lives, and to make decisions that may hurt us or others down the road.

The other extreme is those who are too heavenly minded to be any earthly good. These people tend to spend too much time pursuing spiritual activities and neglecting the physcial and social activities. They tend to have trouble relating the spiritual truths found in God's Word to everyday life because they lack the balance needed to live a balanced life. How is your spiritual balance?

This week as you study the devotional passages, write out a normal weeks schedule from the time you get up to the time you go to bed. How's your life balanced? Are you spending too much time socially and not enough mentally? Write out a revised schedule that you will try to live by for next week. Make this schedule more balanced.

Sunday _____ Read <u>Eccl. 3:1-4</u> _____
          (Date)

How does it apply to my life? _____

Monday _____ Read <u>Ps. 126:1-6</u> _____
          (Date)

Summarize the Passage_____

How does it apply to my life? _____

Tuesday _____ Read <u>John 2:1-2</u> _____
          (Date)

Summarize the Passage_____

How does it apply to my life? _____

Wednesday_____ Read <u>Prov. 23:19-21</u> _____
          (Date)

Summarize the Passage_____

How does it apply to my life? _____

Thursday _____ Read <u>Gal. 5:16, 22-26</u> _____
          (Date)

Summarize the Passage_____

How does it apply to my life? _____

Friday_____ Read <u>Matt. 23:1-5, 23-28</u> _____
          (Date)

Summarize the Passage_____

How does it apply to my life? _____

Saturday_____ Read <u>2 Peter 1:3-11</u> _____
          (Date)

Summarize the Passage_____

How does it apply to my life? _____

Balancing Your Life, Part 2

Don't Give Up

Someone once said we only have one life and it will soon pass, only what's done for Christ will last. In this last devotion of this booklet I want to encourage you to continue on in your Christian walk.

I know hundreds of teens who started living for Christ and after a while gave into the lusts of the flesh. Some left for physical pleasures, some for material pleasures, and some left for mental pursuits, but all forsook the Christian beliefs that were once dear to them.

I also know teens who applied God's Word to their lives and are living victorious lives in the secular workplace, in full-time Christian service, and in the military. God can use you too, if you'll dedicate your life to him.

Take these last four principles and write them in your Bible:

1. *Don't Give Up:* The Christian life is not an easy road, in fact it is a difficult road. Many people start down that road and quickly turn around because of the commitment needed to succeed in Christ. Expect trials, expect temptations, expect blessings, and expect victories.

2. *Don't Give In:* Don't give into temptation. Apply the principles you've learned thoughout the year to your daily life. Strive to be pure in your walk with Christ.

3. *Don't Shut Up:* Continue to be a witness at home, work, school, and play. Your constant low-pressured Christian witness to others can be and will be used mightily by God to win your friends and family to Christ.

4. *Don't Let Satan Win:* Guard your testimony as you would your money from a robber. Don't let Satan get the victory in your life. Commit your life to Christ and live by the principles taught in God's Word.

Where will you be 10 years from now? Will you still be following Christ or will you seek pleasures elsewhere? This week as you read the passages provided, make a commitment to follow Christ no matter where life takes you. Make a commitment to have your devotions and pray every day. Make a commitment to hear those precious words, "well done thou good and faithful servant."

Sunday _____ Read _2 Tim. 4:1-8_____
          (Date)

Summarize the Passage_____

_____

How does it apply to my life? _____

Monday _____ Read _Rom. 12:1-2_____
          (Date)

Summarize the Passage_____

_____

How does it apply to my life? _____

Tuesday _____ Read _Eph. 3:13-21_____
          (Date)

Summarize the Passage_____

_____

How does it apply to my life? _____

Wednesday _____ Read _Phil. 3:10-16_____
          (Date)

Summarize the Passage_____

_____

How does it apply to my life? _____

Thursday _____ Read _Heb. 12:1-2; 1 Cor. 9:24-27_
          (Date)

Summarize the Passage_____

_____

How does it apply to my life? _____

Friday _____ Read _1 Cor. 3:12-15_____
          (Date)

Summarize the Passage_____

_____

How does it apply to my life? _____

Saturday _____ Read _Col. 3:1-17_____
          (Date)

Summarize the Passage_____

_____

How does it apply to my life? _____

Don't Give Up

Prayer Guide

Sunday Prayer Guide

How to Pray

Adoration: worshipping God
Confession: confessing all known and unknown sins
Thanksgiving: thanking God for salvation, for forgiveness, for His blessings
Supplication: praying for my needs and the needs of others

Prayer Requests

For Myself

- Cory's man interview higher job pv.

- student here anorexia

For Others

- bible study grads or people who cant make it

- 2 local fam. lost father & son to suicide 2 different

- Mariam Hoffman stroke

Praises/Answers to Prayer

Monday Prayer Guide

How to Pray

Adoration: worshipping God
Confession: confessing all known and unknown sins
Thanksgiving: thanking God for salvation, for forgiveness, for His blessings
Supplication: praying for my needs and the needs of others

Prayer Requests

For Myself   *For Others*

_____   _____
_____   _____
_____   _____
_____   _____
_____   _____
_____   _____
_____   _____
_____   _____
_____   _____
_____   _____

Praises/Answers to Prayer

_____   _____
_____   _____
_____   _____
_____   _____
_____   _____
_____   _____
_____   _____
_____   _____
_____   _____

Tuesday Prayer Guide

How to Pray

Adoration: worshipping God
Confession: confessing all known and unknown sins
Thanksgiving: thanking God for salvation, for forgiveness, for His blessings
Supplication: praying for my needs and the needs of others

Prayer Requests

For Myself   *For Others*

_____   _____
_____   _____
_____   _____
_____   _____
_____   _____
_____   _____
_____   _____
_____   _____
_____   _____
_____   _____
_____

Praises/Answers to Prayer

_____   _____
_____   _____
_____   _____
_____   _____
_____   _____
_____   _____
_____   _____
_____   _____
_____   _____

Wednesday Prayer Guide

How to Pray

Adoration: worshipping God
Confession: confessing all known and unknown sins
Thanksgiving: thanking God for salvation, for forgiveness, for His blessings
Supplication: praying for my needs and the needs of others

Prayer Requests

For Myself   *For Others*

_____   _____
_____   _____
_____   _____
_____   _____
_____   _____
_____   _____
_____   _____
_____   _____
_____   _____
_____   _____

Praises/Answers to Prayer

_____   _____
_____   _____
_____   _____
_____   _____
_____   _____
_____   _____
_____   _____
_____   _____

Thursday Prayer Guide

How to Pray

Adoration: worshipping God
Confession: confessing all known and unknown sins
Thanksgiving: thanking God for salvation, for forgiveness, for His blessings
Supplication: praying for my needs and the needs of others

Prayer Requests

For Myself   *For Others*

_____   _____
_____   _____
_____   _____
_____   _____
_____   _____
_____   _____
_____   _____
_____   _____
_____   _____
_____   _____

Praises/Answers to Prayer

_____   _____
_____   _____
_____   _____
_____   _____
_____   _____
_____   _____
_____   _____
_____   _____
_____   _____

Friday Prayer Guide

How to Pray

Adoration: worshipping God
Confession: confessing all known and unknown sins
Thanksgiving: thanking God for salvation, for forgiveness, for His blessings
Supplication: praying for my needs and the needs of others

Prayer Requests

For Myself   *For Others*

_____   _____
_____   _____
_____   _____
_____   _____
_____   _____
_____   _____
_____   _____
_____   _____
_____   _____
_____   _____
_____

Praises/Answers to Prayer

_____   _____
_____   _____
_____   _____
_____   _____
_____   _____
_____   _____
_____   _____
_____   _____

Saturday Prayer Guide

How to Pray

Adoration: worshipping God
Confession: confessing all known and unknown sins
Thanksgiving: thanking God for salvation, for forgiveness, for His blessings
Supplication: praying for my needs and the needs of others

Prayer Requests

For Myself   *For Others*

_____   _____
_____   _____
_____   _____
_____   _____
_____   _____
_____   _____
_____   _____
_____   _____
_____   _____
_____   _____

Praises/Answers to Prayer

_____   _____
_____   _____
_____   _____
_____   _____
_____   _____
_____   _____
_____   _____
_____   _____
_____   _____